"Through real-life, everyday e
you new understanding of the
in the Holy Spirit."

Joyce Meyer, Bib _____ ...selling author

"*Heavenly Help* is a really practical look at who the Holy Spirit is in our daily living. I encourage you to read this with an open heart to experience and receive fresh insight from the river of life Himself."

Darlene Zschech, worship leader

"I have seen God do amazing things through the Holy Spirit. I'm excited that Sarah is embracing this journey and sharing her findings about the Holy Spirit with a new generation that needs to know the depth and power of God. Read it and be transformed."

Christine Caine, founder, The A21 Campaign;
bestselling author, *Undaunted*

"Sarah Bowling's passion for God is evident in this poignant reminder that the Holy Spirit is ever-present to help us with the minor and major issues of everyday living. The engaging stories, challenging questions and relevant Scriptures remove the mystery and motivate us to embrace—rather than fear—this empowering force."

Deborah Smith Pegues, international speaker;
bestselling author, *30 Days to Taming Your Tongue*

"In *Heavenly Help*, Sarah Bowling shares from her personal journey of following Jesus and encountering the Holy Spirit. You will be challenged, provoked and awakened through these pages."

Margaret Feinberg, author, *Wonderstruck*

"The Holy Spirit is the most important Person on earth—everyone needs to know Him! Thank you, Sarah, for being moved by compassion and bold enough to proclaim the truth about the Spirit of Truth, the Holy Spirit! I pray that all who read this book will be transformed eternally."

CeCe Winans, gospel singer; multiple
Grammy and Dove Award winner

"Sarah Bowling dares to tackle the charismatic elephant in the room. In a time when clear teaching on the Holy Spirit is so rare, Bowling not only rises to the challenge, but with laser-like precision shines biblical light on the practical function of the Holy Spirit in the life of a believer. Bowling transparently walks us through her own life experiences and takes us on her personal journey from cynicism to clarity and from skeptic to advocate. This is a life-changing book."

Chris Hill, senior pastor, The Potter's House of Denver

"Sarah Bowling helps us to see the Holy Spirit as our Helper, based on Jesus' teaching. Her insights are very practical for both evangelicals and charismatics and are grounded in the Bible. When you read this book, you will see that the Holy Spirit is neither flaky nor retired in our modern world!"

Dr. R. T. Kendall, bestselling author; minister
(retired), Westminster Chapel, London

"Sarah Bowling has hit it out of the park with *Heavenly Help*. Her vulnerability regarding growing up in the charismatic movement alone is worth the read. This is a must-read!"

Robby Dawkins, international conference speaker and
equipper; author, *Do What Jesus Did* and *Identity Thief*

"There are few people I can think of who are as anointed to teach about the Holy Spirit than my friend Sarah Bowling. She has spent her life searching and dissecting God's Word to discover truths that can help all of us live victoriously on this earth. *Heavenly Help* is a book for Christians to learn how to tap into the power of the Holy Spirit every single day so that we can become all God has called us to be. Sarah's down-to-earth, humorous and sometimes very candid approach to the Holy Spirit makes this a great read—easy to understand whether you've just come to believe or have been walking with God for a very long time."

Wendy Treat, senior pastor, Christian Faith Center

"As the daughter of Marilyn Hickey, Sarah comes from a rich heritage of teaching and proclaiming the Word of God. She is a great teacher in her own right and has written a refreshing and modern insight into who the Holy Spirit is and how He functions in today's world. This book will compel you to invite the Holy Spirit into your daily life and let Him upgrade your thoughts, relationships, priorities, decisions and values so that you can make an eternal difference in today's world. It's a great resource for anyone who wants to take their walk with Jesus to the next level."

Dr. Frank Damazio, lead pastor, City Bible Church;
chairman, Ministers Fellowship International;
author, Strategic Church and Strategic Vision

"Many years ago I came into a deeper experience with the Holy Spirit because I read John 14–16, where Jesus taught so much about the Person and work of the Holy Spirit in our lives. So I got really excited when I heard that Sarah Bowling was writing a book about those incredible passages in John's gospel. No one explains the Holy Spirit better than Jesus! And I know that Sarah's book is going to help many people experience His power, His comforting presence and His intimate counsel. You will love this book!"

J. Lee Grady, director, The Mordecai Project; author, Fearless Daughters of the Bible and The Holy Spirit Is Not for Sale

"Sarah Bowling offers a clear-eyed and biblical perspective on the Person and operation of the Holy Spirit. With refreshing honesty and candor, Sarah shares from her own personal experiences with the charismatic movement as well as her path toward embracing the move of the Holy Spirit in her own life. If you have questions about the purpose and function of the third Person of the Trinity, or if you want to give God a more active role in your own life, this book will greatly minister to you."

Jonathan Wiggins, senior pastor, Resurrection Fellowship

"Sarah's insights on the Person of the Holy Spirit will awaken the hearts of all who read this life-giving book. Sarah's love for the Person of the Holy Spirit is contagious. A timely book as we live in the age of the Holy Spirit."

Jude Fouquier, lead pastor, The City Church

"From her unusual vantage point as the daughter of one of America's best-known female evangelists, Sarah Bowling bravely takes on the task of speaking honestly about her struggles to understand the true work of the Holy Spirit. I recommend the book to all who are on the same journey."

Mark Rutland, founder and president, Global Servants

"Sarah Bowling's practical and authentic approach to the Holy Spirit is sure to liberate the reader into a new level of intimacy with God. *Heavenly Help* is filled with biblical insights and personal stories as well as challenging questions to help each person step into a new understanding and a deeper experience. The honesty and integrity of this book will have great impact on all who read it."

Bill Johnson, senior leader, Bethel Church, Redding,
California; bestselling author, *When Heaven Invades
Earth* and *The Power That Changes the World*

Heavenly Help

Heavenly Help

Experiencing the Holy Spirit in Everyday Life

SARAH BOWLING

Chosen

a division of Baker Publishing Group
Minneapolis, Minnesota

Published by Chosen Books
11400 Hampshire Avenue South
Bloomington, Minnesota 55438
www.chosenbooks.com

Chosen Books is a division of
Baker Publishing Group, Grand Rapids, Michigan

Printed in the United States of America

Library of Congress Control Number: 2015956724

ISBN 978-0-8007-9688-4

Cover design by Dual Identity

Author is represented by Fresh Impact PR Group

16 17 18 19 20 21 22   7 6 5 4 3 2 1

I dedicate this book to my mom,
Marilyn Hickey, in gratitude for her
passion for the Bible and the way she has
always encouraged me to go for it.
Thanks, Mom!

Contents

Acknowledgments

I would like to thank my husband and kids, who were far beyond patient with me as I worked on this project—no more painting anytime soon! Thanks, as well, to my friends and co-workers who helped me in ways too numerous to count here: Heidi, Denny, Jane, Stephen, Megan, Ruth, David Holland, Joe, Pastor Jim Pope, Pat, Diane and Menelik.

Thanks to R. T. Kendall for his mentoring investment in me over many years. I am indebted to you, dear friend.

Most of all, thanks to the Helper for drawing me close, eagerly awaiting our daily fellowship.

1

A Fresh Start

May not a single moment of my life be spent
outside the light, love and joy of God's presence.
And not a moment without the entire surrender
of myself as a vessel for Him to fill full of His
Spirit and His love.

ANDREW MURRAY

The earth was formless and void, and darkness
was over the surface of the deep, and the Spirit of
God was moving over the surface of the waters.

GENESIS 1:2

"Stop and listen, and God will show you!"

Out of the mouths of babes can sometimes come divine
wisdom, and my four-year-old son was God's mouthpiece
to me in that moment.

I was searching the house for my purse at 4:10 on a Friday afternoon. All three kids were loaded into their car seats, and I was trying to make it to a 4:30 doctor's appointment for the one I suspected had an ear infection. I wanted to get him to the doctor before the weekend, just in case we would need to start him on an antibiotic.

I was more than a little frantic in that moment, however. My purse had our health insurance card in it, and I had been looking for no less than twenty minutes to find it, with no luck. My frenzied search was leading me straight into the freak-out zone when my son—normally mellow and collected—let God speak to me through him.

His voice caught my attention enough that I sat down in the car, paused and prayed. Then I listened to hear any direction the Helper might give me.

My kids were quiet. (They were likely nervous about the impending meltdown I was about to unleash into our afternoon.) Their stillness allowed me to hear the directive to call the ice-cream shop where we had stopped for a snack earlier that day.

I rang the shop, and sure enough, they had a purse. When I described my purse to them, they were certain it was mine. I zipped over there, collected my treasure and made it on time to the appointment. Whew!

I have just shared with you an example of what it is like to receive divine help in an earthly context. It is my experience that the Holy Spirit offers this help to us—and boatloads more. It is my lifelong experience that the heavenly Helper not only wants to connect with you, but also to participate in your daily living—to give you divine help in ways you have yet to experience.

Throughout my life, the Holy Spirit has been preparing me to write this book for you. The journey to help you know the Holy Spirit through this book began in September 2010, when I started an outrageous adventure of studying for a sermon series on John 14–16. In these chapters of John's gospel, Jesus emphasizes the Holy Spirit during His last meal with His closest followers. They are riveting chapters to me because they provide an in-depth teaching on the Person of the Holy Spirit, who is often so mysterious to us. I am eager to share with you the results of my adventure of studying those chapters.

As I will share with you in a later chapter, I grew up in the charismatic tradition. My upbringing included voluminous amounts of teaching about the Holy Spirit, rooted in the book of Acts and Paul's epistles. I learned numerous times about the gifts of the Holy Spirit found in Paul's first letter to the Corinthians, and I heard countless sermons about walking in the Spirit, as taught in Galatians 5. But for whatever reason, I never seemed to hear any teaching about the Holy Spirit from John 14–16, where Jesus introduces the Helper to us with descriptive explanation. I am amped to share these teachings with you.

But I will also be honest with you. As I wrote this book, I was more than a little intimidated by the prospect of expressing truths about the Third Person of the Trinity, the Holy Spirit. It is one thing to write about topics like success, priorities, making our work sacred, raising healthy children or living in a constructive marriage. All of those things are important, for sure. But when I compare those subjects to writing about our heavenly Helper, it feels like a completely different level. I do not want to go astray in anything I say about God or how we relate to and connect with the Helper. I am also intimidated by the diversity of people who will read this book, knowing each person will come to it with his or her own mindset, emotions, doctrinal biases, experiences and predispositions.

I must say, though, that I think a little bit of intimidation can facilitate a healthy level of respect for the Helper. We must live in the tension of healthy respect and integrated intimacy. My prayer is that as you read through this book, your awareness of and appreciation for the Helper will become sharper. I pray this for you because I believe the Triune God wants to connect with us in both deep intimacy and vibrant transformation.

I also want to acknowledge that this can be a tricky subject. When it comes to the Three Persons of the Trinity, God the Father is not an altogether foreign thought. Whether you had an awesome, absent or awful dad, the concept of *father* is a common paradigm in the human experience. Furthermore, it is not much of a stretch for us to conceptually connect with God the Son, whom we know as Jesus. Jesus came and lived among us, experiencing a familiar human life with family, hunger, friends, sleep, pain, joy and grief. These first two Persons of the Trinity are, for these reasons, usually easy to approach and appreciate.

When we begin to talk about God the Holy Spirit, though, everything can get misty super fast. In fact, even bringing up the word *spirit* sets us into a mode of thinking of things ethereal. *Sublimate* is a scientific term for the process where matter transitions directly from a solid phase into a gas, bypassing the liquid state, and that is often what happens when we think about the Holy Spirit. We move directly from a solid concept to something more like dry ice—gas that wafts up and disappears in a few brief seconds.

I pray this book reverses the sublimation process for you when it comes to your experience of the Helper, making what may seem to be an ethereal vapor into a concrete reality.

Here is the road map for our journey. In the next chapter, we will explore Jesus' revolutionary introduction of this Helper to His disciples—what it means for the Holy Spirit to be our heavenly help and how such help is radical. After that, we will learn what it means to encounter the Spirit of truth, how to accept the invitation to live as children rather than orphans, how the Helper reminds us what we need to know, ways we can allow our lives to be witnesses of our God life and how our receiving of the Holy Spirit is actually an upgrade to the experience the disciples knew with Jesus. We will also learn about the gifts and fruits of the Spirit, what happens when we do not let the Helper into our lives in the various ways available to us and what it can look like to lean on this heavenly help every single day of our lives.

Additionally, each chapter ends with two special features. The first is what I call the IRA—and by that, I do not mean a kind of retirement savings account or the Irish Republican Army. Rather, it stands for "Inspect, Reflect, Apply" and is a grouping of questions and exercises that can be helpful for your own self-study or for use in group discussions to reflect and make application of each chapter's content to your daily life. It is my core conviction that the Helper wants to be thoroughly integrated into our daily living so that we live out a beautiful lifestyle of transformation with heavenly help. I pray each of these IRA sections provides practical tools and exercises to make this conviction relevant for you.

Second, each chapter closes with an allegory. I want to help you connect and engage with the Helper on a deeper level than your current status. While some people connect in a more cerebral way, where going into Jesus' words and the Greek and historical contexts behind biblical passages are rich and helpful exercises, other people connect in a more relational or emotional way, finding their deepest connections through spiritual conversations, experiences and interactions. For those of us wired up in this second way, I have included a brief allegory with each chapter that endeavors to link the topic of the chapter with a relational expression found through the interactions of two fictional women I have named Naomi and Ruth.

I chose these names, in part, because of the biblical content found in the book of Ruth, where we find the beautiful forging of a deep and intimate relationship between two women who suffered tremendous loss. Naomi's son Mahlon was the husband of Ruth. When the common link that bound these women together was removed through Mahlon's death, Ruth made the decision to stay attached to Naomi, her mother-in-law. In the book's most-famous passage, Ruth tells her mother-in-law:

> "Do not urge me to leave you or turn back from following you; for where you go, I will go, and where you lodge, I will lodge. Your people shall be my people, and your God, my God. Where you die, I will die, and there I will be buried. Thus may the Lord do to me, and worse, if anything but death parts you and me."
>
> Ruth 1:16–17

The book of Ruth is rich and rewarding, filled with real-life intimacy, hardships, disappointments and satisfaction. Ruth and Naomi cultivate a deep connection through their struggles, uncertainties and fears. They choose to become a mother and daughter to each other, not merely defaulting to their bloodline realities.

I would encourage you to read through the book of Ruth and to consider how the relationship between these two women grew into a permanent, fruitful and intimate connection that brought great life, joy, hope and future. The brief allegorical expressions included at the end of each chapter are meant to make a similar connection. They are intended to help you see how the Helper can become more real in your life, full stop.

So, let's jump into this fantastic adventure. I have lined up some initial questions for your first IRA experience below, and our first allegory story with Ruth and Naomi follows. Then we pick up the trail of our adventure in chapter 2 with an exploration of radical help. Onward!

Inspect, Reflect, Apply

1. What has been your experience of our heavenly Helper, the Holy Spirit?

2. Would you say you are more of a cerebral learner or someone who learns in a more relational and emotional

way? How have you seen evidence of this in your learning experiences?

3. Take some time over the next week or so to read John 14–16, paying special attention to all that Jesus says about the Helper.

Ruth and Naomi: An Introduction

"Ready, set, *go!*"

I jumped off the bridge and plunged toward the ground, wind blowing my hair back and my eyes wider than car tires. My stomach rushed into my throat.

As I plummeted to the ground, I reminded myself the bungee cord was sturdy—hopefully. I'd always wanted to try bungee jumping, and my new friend, Naomi, was waiting on the bridge, next in line for her turn, cheering me on in the plunge.

The earth kept getting closer and closer, and I knew I was reaching the limit of the cord. I kept praying it wouldn't snap on me at the bottom. I could see the headlines now: "Woman Plunges to Her Death."

I brushed aside the pessimism and decided to enjoy the last nanoseconds before the elastic bounced me up and rescued me from a deadly face-plant.

I had hopped into this bungee-jumping adventure after meeting Naomi by the brussels sprouts in the grocery store.

She was mumbling to herself about how a person was supposed to eat those little alien green balls.

To this day, I have no idea why I piped up to tell her, a total stranger in the grocery store, how to cook a freaky vegetable for a tasty outcome. Normally, I don't talk to strangers. More often than not, I think they're strange, and I don't need to add my strange to their strange, thereby making the world altogether more strange. But there I went with my usual "leap then look" strategy, offering up an easy and delicious recipe for brussels sprouts to a total stranger.

And she didn't freak out! In fact, she seemed really happy to have my input, and we started up a friendly conversation, sharing a few cooking ideas as we worked our way through our weekly grocery lists. I learned my new friend's name was Naomi, and I found her interesting and engaging.

The next week, we happened to catch up again in the grocery store and struck up another fun conversation, exchanging more recipes while getting our weekly ration of eggs, milk, lunchmeat and bread. At the end of our shopping foray, Naomi mentioned bungee jumping as something she'd been wanting to try for years. She had finally worked up the courage to take the dive with a friend.

"I thought I'd ask you," she explained, "because you seem kind of unconventional. Maybe you're just crazy enough to enjoy new adventures!"

Little did Naomi know that *unconventional* is my middle name—almost.

We exchanged phone numbers in the parking lot, and that's how I found myself in this precarious and playful plunge, plummeting through the air and diving into a new friendship.

After I finished my jump, I climbed up on the bridge and described the adrenaline rush.

"Oh my gosh," I exclaimed. "That was totally awesome! I was so scared and exhilarated, all at the same time. I haven't experienced that kind of a rush in years. Let's do it again!"

The more I talked, the more Naomi's face became focused. In a strange way, describing my experience to her seemed to draw us closer, making us feel more connected.

"Do you have any suggestions for me with this adventure?" she asked. "I've never done anything like this, and it seems you had an incredible experience. Tell me what I should know."

It didn't seem Naomi was getting cold feet by asking me this. Instead, she seemed to want me to share as much of my experience with her as I could. She had paid a sizable amount of money and put a lot of effort into checking this adventure off her bucket list, so learning from my experience was going to help ensure her success with it.

Still, since we were new friends, I wasn't sure whether to tell her how scared I had been. Was it better to stay solely on the encouragement track with this?

I looked at the clear sky and then replied, "Naomi, this is the perfect day and perfect situation for you to do this. I'll be honest—I was definitely scared as I put on the safety harness and stepped up to the platform. How could I not be? But once I jumped, the rush was worth the fear. You're going to *love* this experience! I suggest you think only of what you need to do next. Put on the safety harness one leg at a time, and then let the instructor help you get ready. This will be a blast!"

I'm at my best when I get to encourage people, and Naomi was giving me the opportunity to be my best self. While I'm a fiercely independent person and enjoy adventures like bungee jumping, I'm also intensely loyal. Getting to affirm and coach Naomi in this challenging moment allowed me to build a deeper friendship with her.

She looked at me with eager eyes as she slipped on the safety harness. The instructor clipped the cord to her harness and gave her a few more instruction points. Then she stepped to the edge of the bridge.

"Don't look—just leap!" I yelled.

Naomi looked at me and offered a knowing little smirk before taking the plunge.

And that is how my rich, deep and amazing friendship with Naomi moved from the produce section of the grocery store to a trust that can hold the thoughts, feelings and fullness of my heart.

2

Radical Help

Anytime you see a turtle up on top of a fence
post, you know he had some help.

ALEX HALEY

"I will ask the Father, and He will give you another Helper, that He may be with you forever."

JOHN 14:16

Our conversation about heavenly help starts with Jesus'
words in John 14:16: "I will ask the Father, and He will give
you another Helper, that He may be with you forever." These
words launch us into a radical and supernatural adventure
with the Holy Spirit. With this brief sentence, Jesus introduces His closest and last followers to the most important
next step in their relationship with Him.

For some brief context, Jesus' introduction to this heavenly
help is found during the Last Supper, an essential discourse

at the end of His earthly existence. Here is what is happening the night Jesus shares this Last Supper with His disciples: Judas has left the dinner to meet up with the religious leaders so he can work out a plan to betray Jesus. Jesus knows He and His disciples will head to the Garden of Gethsemane soon, where He will pray to surrender His will to the Father and His sweat will be like drops of blood. He knows about Judas' betrayal. He knows He will be crucified. He knows all of His followers will be scattered and abandon Him.

Ultimately, Jesus knows this Last Supper is the final time He will be with His closest friends in a place of such intimacy, vulnerability and connection. This is the time He chooses to introduce them to the heavenly Helper. He knows they are going to need the Holy Spirit if they are going to continue being His followers.

With this context in mind, I believe these chapters in John 14–16 are the culmination of Jesus' most important thoughts to His closest followers. They were not offered to the fickle masses, the treacherous religious leaders or the political zealots. They were given to the followers who had been with Him the longest and were His most intimate friends.

Up to this point, Jesus had only briefly mentioned the Holy Spirit to His followers. For instance, in Luke 11:13, He says, "If you then, being evil, know how to give good gifts to your children, how much more will your heavenly Father give the Holy Spirit to those who ask Him?" And in John 3:5, He says, "Truly, truly, I say to you, unless one is born of water and the Spirit he cannot enter the kingdom of God."

But in John 14–16, Jesus says so much more. He teaches His closest followers who the Helper is, and He starts in John

14:16: "I will ask the Father, and He will give you another Helper, that He may be with you forever."

When I began to study this verse, I was riveted not only by its simplicity, but also by its depth. Jesus says so much in this one sentence. He starts on a simple level and slowly walks us deeper and deeper into our discovery.

To begin, this verse is a direct affirmation of who the Trinity is:

- Father: "I will ask the Father"
- Son: "I," spoken by Jesus
- Holy Spirit: "another Helper"

The reality that the Helper is part of our Triune God is important. The Holy Spirit is not a kind of second-string deity, nor is the Holy Spirit like Jesus' optional accessory. The Helper is on the same level of importance as God the Father and God the Son.

Furthermore, when Jesus asks for "another" Helper, the word in Greek that Jesus uses is interesting. In Greek, two words can be used for *another*. The first is *hetero*, which means "having a different quality, or dissimilar." This is a Greek word that gets used in the English language for words like *heterogeneous, heterosexual, heterodoxy* and more.

But when Jesus speaks of "another Helper," He uses the Greek word *allon*, which means "the same quality, or a similar type." In other words, Jesus is saying He will ask the Father to give His followers a similar type of Helper, implying that Jesus has been helping them for the past two to three years and would ask the Father to send a similar kind of Helper to them.

Another interesting thing that catches my attention in this verse is that Jesus does not give the Holy Spirit a formal introduction. He does not say to His disciples, "I am going to ask the Father to give you the Third Person of the Trinity, God the Spirit, also known as the Holy Spirit. Make sure you get His name right—first name *Holy*, last name *Spirit*."

Instead, in Jesus' primary introduction of the Holy Spirit, He uses something more like a nickname, using a common term found throughout the New Testament and in Greek literature. It is the term *parakaletos*. In Greek, this is a compound word—*para*, meaning "alongside or besides," and *kaleo*, meaning "to call or beckon." When these words are combined, their meaning can include someone who is an advocate, comforter, counselor, helper or even assistant. It has lots of different meanings and applications and, again, is common in the Greek language.

In my thinking, Jesus chose the word *parakaletos* for exactly these reasons. Let us consider the possibility that Jesus meant for us to understand the Holy Spirit first and foremost as our Helper. Perhaps we could even call the Holy Spirit our professional help. Additionally, because the term *parakaleo* or *parakletos* has so many different meanings and applications, perhaps Jesus wanted us to understand that the Helper is not intended to be known only as a formal title but rather as a more universal connection and application to our lives in the context of help. The word *help*, in itself, is a broad word, isn't it?

At the end of Jesus' introduction, let us not overlook that Jesus says the Helper will always be with us, all the time. This says to you and me that the Helper is continually present and that we always have access to supernatural help, 24/7. If it's two a.m., you have access to supernatural help. I you're in Kathmandu, divine help is readily available to you. Let's be mindful that Jesus told us the Helper will be with us all the time, and this means that we have a divine "help desk" available all the time and in every situation, ready for the asking!

How We Are Helped

I have had some really amazing experiences with the Helper. He has done some cool stuff in my daily life. One time, my husband and I took our oldest son and his best friend for a one-day ski trip to celebrate our son's twelfth birthday. Because we live in Denver, it is convenient for us to pop up to the mountains for a quick day of skiing and then head back home for dinner.

As we had done hundreds of times before, we were driving up our normal road. This time, however, we hit an icy patch and my husband pretty much lost control of the car. We began to slide perpendicular to the road and into the oncoming traffic.

I immediately yelled, "Help!" and began to pray really hard.

If you can believe it, we dodged all of the oncoming traffic, including a semitruck, and slid off the other side of the road into a snowbank, almost into a mini-forest. When we finally came to a stop, our car was lodged in the snowbank at a 45-degree angle. No one was hurt.

Long story short, the tow truck extracted our car from the snow and got it back on the road, and we drove off to continue our son's birthday celebration on the ski slopes (even though all of our legs were a little shaky!).

Here is another example. Recently, I had an appointment at an office building and had to use a parking meter for my car. When I put the money in the meter, I heard this little voice on the inside tell me to add an extra fifty cents. I ignored the voice, even though I heard it several times. Sure enough, when I finished my appointment and came to my car, I had a $25 parking ticket that I could have avoided had I listened to the Helper's voice and added the extra fifty cents to the meter.

In another example, I had an experience a year after my dad died that was super helpful and comforting. While my dad's passing was not premature or unexpected, his death was nevertheless a great loss to me. A little more than a year after his death, I found myself joining in an outreach with one of my friends. It happened around the same time as the first anniversary of my dad's death, and my friend and I remembered that we had been at the same outreach the previous year.

My mindset the previous year had been grim, to put it mildly, given its proximity to the loss of my dad. At that time, I was just trying to keep myself together and not fall apart, into a big puddle of tears, during the event. A year later, though, I could see the many ways the Helper had strengthened me and helped me grow. I could also see ways the Helper had filled in some of the gaps I had felt from losing my dad.

I have also had many occasions of experiencing divine help with keeping my mouth shut when I wanted to rip someone's head off. I have had divine help with my kids, knowing when to say important things and how to ask strategic questions. I have had lots of help in my marriage, in my workplace, in my various volunteer capacities and even in mundane things, like grocery shopping and running kids to events and activities. Even writing this book is a great adventure for me in the world of help!

I do not know what your experience of needing and receiving help might be, but I can say for myself that as a kid, I was extremely independent and was almost insulted when people tried to help me. Clearly, this was not a great thing, and thankfully, as I have aged, I have become less independent—kind of. If the truth be known, I can acknowledge I need immeasurable help, even though it is a challenge for me to actually receive it. Nevertheless, I am better at welcoming help today than I was in the past, and I continue to make progress in this area. God is helping me become increasingly comfortable with my need for help, and I am becoming more and more aware that help is a wonderful context through which we can experience greater intimacy and communion with God.

One of the things that I find to be valuable is to frame the idea of help in a divine context—to frame it as heavenly help. When I think about God helping me, I am quick to acknowledge that I desperately need such divine help threaded through my existence.

Here are a few ways I need help. Perhaps you can relate. I need help to:

- Be a good wife, mother, daughter, friend, leader and human.
- Drive with greater courtesy.

- Be kind to myself and to the people with whom I interact throughout any given day.
- Make decisions that are constructive and healthy.
- Plan for the future.
- Accurately assess the past.
- Think truthfully about things that can be emotionally cloudy for me.
- Not always say what I am thinking.
- Wisely spend money for purposeful outcomes.
- Keep healthy routines in my daily living, including exercise, Bible and prayer time, eating wisely and balancing time with achievements.
- Maintain healthy relationships, boundaries, seasons and interactions.
- Remember stuff (the list is too long for me to remember).

The more I think about where and how I need help, the more I recognize that I am a needy person who needs lots of it. And when we talk about needing help as it relates to the Holy Spirit—our professional and divine form of help—this means nothing less than 100 percent joy, fellowship, truth and glorious freedom are ours. Receiving help from the Holy Spirit is living an abundant life!

How It Is Radical

Lastly, let's think about the way having the Holy Spirit as our heavenly help can help us live radical lives. Because let's face it: The world in which we live needs some radical living. Such radical living is strongly countercultural.

For example, if you think about it, being radical does not mean being impatient, because the world in which we live is impatient. Consider how many times you have stopped the microwave early because you wanted the popcorn to be ready *now*.

Another thing that is not radical in our world is being unkind. There is plenty of unkindness running around, but being kind can be extremely radical. Recently, I was in a coffee shop chatting with the cashier. We were having a nice talk, and she made the observation that I was kind and gracious, "like a breath of fresh air." In her thinking, my kindness was radical, compared to her other customers, even though it did not feel radical to me.

Being depressed, tired, discouraged and even hopeless is not radical in our world, either. Instead, it seems rather common. Other things commonly found in our world include apathy, anxiety, lack of commitment and being out of control, to name just a few.

But here is the real scoop on what radical can look like. Radical character in this world is about being faithful and committed instead of flaky and uncommitted. Radical character is full of peace and joy, as opposed to being anxious and depressed. It is radical in our world to genuinely love without the deception or selfish interests that commonly corrupt what is generally accepted as love.

If I come straight to the point about what radical looks like, it is the list Paul gives us in Galatians 5:22–23 about the fruit of the Spirit. In our world, living radical is all about living with love, joy, peace, patience, kindness, goodness, faithfulness, gentleness and self-control. In today's world, these characteristics are radical.

Now, the Holy Spirit also helps us live supernaturally, which is another form of radical living. This word *supernatural* can get wonky for us really fast, though. We often get our ideas about the supernatural from special effects in Hollywood movies. Think about the many amazing but unrealistic things we watch on TV, the Internet and in movies. For example, there is that scene in *The Empire Strikes Back* where Yoda lifts Luke Skywalker's starfighter from the swamp by using The Force. If we are not careful, we can think Yoda's trick was somehow supernatural, when in reality it was nothing more than special effects.

We can also be misguided about the supernatural due to our skepticism. We learn at a young age not to trust or believe everything we hear or see, and if we are not careful, our culture can seduce us into being better skeptics than believers. Its influence can shape us to dismiss the supernatural through rationalization, cynicism, sarcasm, arrogance and outright rejection of whatever cannot be explained with our intellectual understanding.

In contrast to our intellectual and rational world, the Bible overflows with witness to the radically supernatural, all of which squarely aligns with what the Holy Spirit can do. Indeed, Genesis 1 is the cosmic account of God creating the world in which we live and the Spirit of God moving over the waters (see Genesis 1:2). Continuing through the Old Testament, we read about fire falling from heaven, leprosy being healed, the Red Sea parting and much more.

Plenty of supernatural happenings show up in the New Testament as well, starting with the virgin birth of Jesus and continuing all the way through to the book of Revelation. It is especially incredible to read about all of the radically supernatural things that happen in the book of Acts, with the apostle Paul being one of the leading examples of someone living out the supernatural adventures of life spent with our heavenly Helper.

Speaking of the apostle Paul, he goes on to describe the supernatural and radical gifts of the Holy Spirit in 1 Corinthians 12. These gifts, or expressions, include words of wisdom, words of knowledge, miracles, prophecy, healing, faith, discernment of spirits, speaking in tongues and interpreting tongues. I would suggest to you that these gifts, especially in our world, are radical because of their supernatural demonstration. (I will talk about these gifts in greater detail in chapter 9.)

To get right down to it, when Jesus introduces His disciples to the Helper as the Third Person of the Trinity, what a comforting, encouraging, practical and radical connection He gives us to God, who longs to be at work in our practical, earthly and daily living. In the course of this book, I want to show you how the Helper will comfort and encourage you, making a transforming connection between you and God.

I have to admit, I did not always feel this way. In fact, in my younger years, I was repelled by people who were trying to "conjure up" the Holy Spirit. Sometimes it felt like various demonstrations of the Holy Spirit were nothing more than thinly disguised human manipulation.

How did I get from that place to where I am today, rejoicing in the Helper and enjoying greater intimacy, connection and communion with God through Him? Let me tell you the story in our next chapter.

Inspect, Reflect, Apply

1. Do you consider yourself to be a highly independent person, or can you readily accept help?

2. How do you think other people see you—as highly independent or open to receiving help?

3. How have you received help from the Holy Spirit?

4. What are some areas where being independent has undermined or compromised the Helper working in your life?

5. List a few experiences in your life that you would describe as radical. In what ways did these experiences shape your thinking and subsequent decisions?

"Help!"

"Would you like some help?" the voice above me said.

I was on my stomach, face squashed into the snow, and I could feel a shooting pain in my shoulder.

"No, thanks," I said, my voice muffled by the snow. "I think I can get up on my own."

I tried to lift myself, but the pain threw me into the debilitated zone. *Great.* I couldn't lift myself, and now some stranger was offering to help me—a nightmare combination for me, the fiercely independent and "do it myself" poster child.

Naomi is a skier, and I snowboard. We'd decided to drop the kids off at school and zip up to the mountains for a couple hours of fun before I had to be back in "mom mode."

Needless to say, my getting injured hadn't been part of our game plan for the day. We were just beginning to enjoy some awesome snow when I caught an edge on my snowboard and slammed into the mountain, landing with all of my weight on my shoulder.

Naomi was already ahead of me on the ski run, so I was at the mercy of some stranger asking me if I wanted help.

Do I want help? No!

Do I *need* help? Well . . . man, I was in a jam. I most definitely didn't want some strange man helping me in my current condition, but I absolutely *needed* help.

I thanked him for his offer but mumbled that I had a friend I could call. He still waited. So I fumbled around in my coat, found my phone and called Naomi.

In an uncertain and scared voice, I said, "Hey, friend, I've taken a fall, and I think I've hurt myself pretty bad. Would you be able to come and help me?"

Asking for help sticks in my throat worse than peanut butter coating your tongue, and I most certainly didn't want to get help from the strange man who was waiting for my friend to come to my aid. After a little bit, Naomi showed up, and we made our way down the slope and over to the medical building, where they determined that I'd dislocated my shoulder.

After a few pain meds, Naomi stayed with me as they "reduced" my shoulder—that's medical lingo for popping the ball back into the socket—with a fair amount of cajoling and "helpful" coercion.

And so began all of the "help" questions:

"Would you like help with your shirt?"

"Would you please help me pick up the kids from school?"

"Would you please help me to unload the groceries from the car?"

"Can I help you put your suitcase in the overhead bin on this plane?"

Help was becoming my middle name, and I was getting more and more cranky by the day as I watched my independence erode and decay through the onslaught of my need and dependence. I loathed the idea of needing help—until I had a transforming conversation with Naomi.

One afternoon, I invited Naomi over to have some tasty coffee and enjoy some fun conversation—one of my absolute favorite things to do. She was sitting at the counter in the kitchen, and I was trying to unload the dishwasher. I was having a really difficult time with the dishes because my shoulder was throbbing with pain.

"Why don't you ask for help?" Naomi asked.

I recoiled because I hate any kind of conversation that makes me feel weak, vulnerable or frail. I grew up as a latchkey kid, so help is as alien to me as snow on a beach in Florida. It's virtual nonsense. My friend was asking what seemed to be an innocent question, but for me it was charged with buckshot.

"Asking for help makes me feel weak and dependent," I told her. "I don't like to ask for help because I've always prized independence, even as a little girl."

I could tell Naomi was thinking about my answer. Based on the contorted look of her face, though, I could see she was reflecting on something that bothered her.

"When you're independent," she finally said, "do you ever think about how that might affect someone else?"

"Of course," I replied. "Whenever I ask someone for help, I'm imposing on them and taking some of their valuable time and energy. Furthermore, I grew up in a family where independence was a premium value and applauded with generous affirmation and rewards. Besides, only weak people need help."

"Ouch! No wonder you don't have many friends," Naomi said. "You're judgmental, arrogant and isolationist. How on earth did your husband ever get beyond your independence to endure more than twenty years of marriage?"

41

Here I thought being independent was a strength, but Naomi was upending that idea and exposing it as a weakness—at best. More realistically, it was being shown to be a hindrance to connecting with someone in authenticity and vulnerability.

As Naomi picked up some glasses to put back in the cupboard, I found myself fumbling for words. All I could say at that point was, "Hmmmmm."

She kept unloading the dishwasher, putting the silverware away, along with the bowls and coffee cups. The room was pregnant with quiet, as though anticipating some kind of thoughtful engagement, but I was too stunned for words and kind of hurt by her insightful honesty.

What do you say to a person who holds up a mirror, forcing you to look at some ugliness you've accessorized in gaudy costume jewelry and high-grade deception?

Since she was on a roll, Naomi went on.

"Ruth, I also think you idolize your independence because it keeps a buffer between you and any deeper friendships or relationships. Is it possible you might be afraid of being transparent or vulnerable? Are you afraid of being hurt? Are there lingering pains you haven't forgiven, so you protect yourself in the cloak of independence, pretending that it's Kevlar, making you invincible? Maybe your Kevlar is more like Superman's kryptonite."

And on that happy note, I decided I wasn't interested in continuing the conversation—at least not on this topic—so I adjusted our discussion to something more shallow and superficial.

"Did you catch that new brussels sprouts recipe by the sample display while shopping last week?" I asked. "I tried it, and it was totally disgusting—no one in my family could gag down even half a mouthful! Sometimes I think these food distributors are totally clueless about cooking and how food should taste."

"Nice change of subject, Ruth. Did I hit a nerve or say something that was difficult for you to hear?"

Everything inside me was screaming, *Are you kidding me? Who do you think you are, and what makes you think you can call me out like that? I don't know you well enough to have this level of transparency or exposure. This is no bueno!*

Instead of letting my mouth fly with these thoughts, I simply replied, "Well, you've certainly brought up some interesting ideas, and I probably need some time to think about your observations. I'll get back to you later about this."

Since my efforts to change the subject didn't work, I was now trying the stall tactic to see if I could throw her onto a different timeline for discussing it.

It didn't work.

"Ruth, I think you're stalling," she said, "and while I can appreciate that you might want some time to think about the whole independence paradigm, you need to understand that if you'd like to be close friends with me, you'll have to let down your guard, let me be who I am and let me help you. When you resist my help, you resist me, and we'll never be as good friends as we can be when you don't give me the freedom to be my helpful self in your daily living."

And that's how we came to a trust juncture every friendship tests. I just hoped I could learn how to pass through it with Naomi.

3

Lots of Unusual

O Holy Spirit . . . descend plentifully into my
heart; enlighten the dark corners of this neglected
dwelling, and scatter there thy cheerful beams!

SAINT AUGUSTINE

"The Spirit of God has made me, and the breath
of the Almighty gives me life."

JOB 33:4

I am a pastor's kid, and I grew up in the heyday of the charismatic renewal—a time in the 1970s and 1980s when there
was a strong emphasis on the Holy Spirit in denominational
churches and a large migration of Christians to more independent and nondenominational churches. Because my dad was

a pastor and my mom, Marilyn Hickey, is a well-known Bible teacher, church was always my second home.

In the charismatic church where I grew up, it was normal for people to speak in tongues, and we welcomed the public expressions of the gifts of the Holy Spirit listed in 1 Corinthians 12. These included the gifts of healing, prophecy, words of knowledge and wisdom and speaking in and interpreting tongues. In my church, these gifts were considered a normal part of a Christian's experience.

Consider my shock, on the first day of my sixth-grade year in my new Lutheran school, when one of the girls in my class whispered in my ear, "I know that you speak in tongues." It was my first awareness of being the odd woman out in this Lutheran school, with the speaking-in-tongues stuff. While everyone was generally kind and respectful, I learned quickly that my beliefs about the gifts of the Holy Spirit were completely uncommon and even unknown among the majority of my classmates.

Needless to say, my Bible teacher and I had some interesting conversations during that school year. Those discussions were helpful to me, though, as I saw a whole new perspective on Christianity that I had never known before. It was a healthy experience for both of us as we dug into our Bibles.

I continued to attend Lutheran schools through twelfth grade, after which I enrolled at Oral Roberts University. There, I attended First United Methodist Church, pastored by Dr. Jimmy Buskirk, and majored in physics for one semester and then German education. When I finished my degree in German, I moved home to teach social studies for almost four years at the Christian school that was part of my parents' church.

During that season, I was not a full-on charismatic, even though my parents were. Truth be known, at that time, I was way more comfortable attending the Lutheran church connected to my junior high school than attending my parents' church. Nevertheless, I would attend their church out of respect for them while also attending a Lutheran service on Sundays.

When I reflect back on those years, I am disappointed in the arrogance I see in my thoughts and interactions. Unfortunately, arrogance can often be the natural bedfellow of intellect, and during this time, along with my arrogance, my Christianity was entirely intellectual. I was repelled by anything I considered emotional or flaky, and if the Bible was mishandled or misquoted, I dismissed the entire message along with the person giving it. I was an intellectual elitist, annoyed, dismissive and intolerant.

Turned Off by Revival

It was during this time that my mom mentioned she was going to a revival service at a nearby church. I found it strange that she would attend a church other than ours on a regular church-service night, so I started to ask some questions.

"How do you know this is a revival?" I asked.

"Well, there are some demonstrations from the Holy Spirit," she replied.

"Like what?"

I could tell she was getting a little nervous at hearing my critical tone, but she said, "Well, some people fall down. Some people get stuck in trances. And there's lots of laughing."

My mind started racing a thousand miles a minute at this point, thinking of what I considered to be those "kooky charismatics." I assumed everything presented at the revival meeting would be emotional and half-baked. I bet there would be lots of Bible verses taken out of context, not to mention flaky doctrine.

Given the spiritual and intellectual journey I had taken the last many years, it was no surprise I responded with such skepticism, disdain and cynicism. And yet due to some genuine experiences in my upbringing, I also knew there was an outside chance this stuff could be legitimate.

For example, when I was fourteen, our youth group attended a summer church camp in Kansas. I remember getting off the bus and looking forward to doing lots of fun stuff, like swimming, river rafting and hiking. When the camp director gave us our introductory tour, I was disappointed to find there was no swimming pool or river and that hiking was going to be a hot and possibly dangerous dance with rattlesnakes. Although the camp had horses, these particular horses looked like they were at their last stop before the glue factory. We were supposed to spend five days there in the Land of Toto—maybe a tornado would throw in some adventure!

Despite this depressing introduction, we managed to have lots of fun that week. What's more, I had a very strong experience with God during one of the evening services, when someone prayed for me and I sensed God's presence powerfully. It was such a dramatic experience that I became incredibly hungry for God. I was able to sense God's presence, voice and direction with a clarity I had never experienced before. It felt like the ranch was thoroughly saturated with God's presence, and I began waking up early to spend time with God by myself in prayer and the Bible. I had a voracious appetite for God that was nothing less than a result of the Holy Spirit working in both my heart and my desires.

As we came to the end of the week and it was time to go home, I felt that I needed to stay another week to continue growing with God. I checked with my parents and the camp director, and everyone gave me the green light to stay an extra week.

Those two weeks had a powerful impact on me, connecting me with God in a supernatural way. When I came home, I was a different person. I was turned on to the power of God. I started to memorize Bible verses and study the Bible for no reason other than my passionate desire to know God better. I was more kind, gentle, obedient, gracious and helpful, not to mention less selfish and reactionary.

One of the things I remember about that summer after the church camp in Kansas was a sensitivity I developed to hearing and feeling God, and it stayed with me every day of that summer. I am thankful to God for that summer. It planted a deep spiritual anchor in my heart during my tumultuous teen years, and it helped keep me spiritually tethered to God when there were lots of opportunities to get detoured.

Coming back to my conversation with my mom about the revival service at that time, I was decidedly less open to the supernatural side of Christianity at that time. Nevertheless, I had enough real experiences of God that I also did not want to miss a genuine opportunity to connect with God. I have since come to the realization that I was repelled by people who were trying to conjure up the Holy Spirit or disguise human manipulation in spiritual garb. But I was never turned off by the actual Holy Spirit. Quite the contrary—if something was genuinely of God, I wanted to be first in line.

Given this truth, a little piece of my thinking held out the chance that this revival thing was the real stuff, even though I thought it highly unlikely. So I continued to question my mom.

"Do you think I'd like the service?" I asked.

"Oh, no," she said. "You would be skeptical."

Well, that solved it for me—I was going. My primary purpose would be to sniff out doctrinal abuses, listen for Scriptures taken out of context and watch for emotional freakiness. After observing those things, I would be in an informed place to reject the whole thing as the usual "kooky charismatic" chicanery.

Again, a tiny voice in my head said, *If this is genuinely the Holy Spirit, then I don't want to miss that—but it's probably not.*

I was in for a surprise.

Surprised by Laughter

So, when you attend a church service with Marilyn Hickey as her guest, you get to sit with her, often in the first few rows of the church. On this particular occasion, I would have preferred to sit in the back to do my critical analysis, but no such luck. We sat in the second row.

I enjoyed the music, and the people were nice. But as the speaker got up to minister, I moved into analysis mode and listened with great intensity for heresy and any mishandling of biblical context. However, as I listened, the speaker did not take anything out of context in the Bible, and I did not smell even a whiff of questionable doctrine.

It became tricky, though, when people around me started to laugh for no apparent reason. They just started laughing. As I watched them out of the corner of my eye, I noticed the laughter stuff seemed to rub off on the other people nearby.

I tried to figure out what was causing this laughter—maybe the speaker was telling a joke, made a funny face that I missed or did something goofy that went over my head. But these people were laughing for a long time, and they laughed longer and harder as time when on until they pretty much seemed outright silly.

As the service continued, the minister kept speaking from his text in the Bible, and more pockets of people kept laughing in the audience. I was trying to look normal and comfortable, but I was totally uncomfortable on the inside.

After the minister had been speaking for a while, he came down from the platform and continued to preach and smile as he walked around. Clearly, he was comfortable with this whole laughing thing. It did not make him jittery in any way.

At one point when he was walking around and preaching, he touched me and my mom on our shoulders, and we both began to laugh, too! As I laughed, I tried to figure out why I was laughing, but I knew this was a genuine experience for me with the Holy Spirit. Having grown up in church, I had enough God experiences to know the difference, and again, I was never opposed to whatever was genuinely God.

What I experienced with the laughing stuff was not humanly contrived. I was far too skeptical and cynical to blindly skip down the path of human deception. It was a divine experience, and I could sense God's presence.

When my mom and I drove home that night, I let her know I would be attending the revival service the following evening. She nodded her head with a smile but did not say anything more.

Moved to Ministry

The next night at the service, I cannot say for sure what happened. All I know is that I had a powerful experience with God. I remember sensing God's presence in a way I never had before, and at one point I found myself on the floor—completely uncharacteristic of me—totally overwhelmed by God's presence.

To this day, I am still at a loss for words to describe my experience that night, except to say that my values and priorities were revolutionized. Before that night, I was intent on getting my doctorate and possibly being a missionary in some foreign country. I was dead set against doing anything in ministry, especially in the United States, because in my thinking, the United States was overflowing with Christianity. I wanted to let God use my talents in places where there was an observable deficiency of the Gospel. After that night, though, I was extremely keen to do ministry and teach the Bible wherever God would open the door.

Some before-and-after contrasts in me as a result of that night include:

Before	After
Arrogant and elitist	Humble and serving
Private with my faith	Openly sharing my faith

Before	After
An intellectual snob	Less critical and more accepting
Condemning and harsh	Forgiving and welcoming

The rest of that week, I went to the revival services because my hunger for God had been reawakened and revitalized at the expense of my arrogance and elitism. To this day, more than twenty years after that revival service, I am keenly hungry for God in my life and for the work of the Holy Spirit.

Which brings us back to the focus of this book. Perhaps you can relate to my posture of skepticism toward anything too Spirit-filled or charismatic. Perhaps you find some intellectual arrogance creeping into your experience of faith that is comforting and unsettling at the same time. Perhaps you wonder what is trustworthy when it comes to the Holy Spirit's interaction and involvement in our lives.

We are going to explore that, so let's stay together for the ride. To begin, we will lay some groundwork about the identity and intent of our heavenly Helper. Then, later in the book, we will tackle some of the more supernatural manifestations of the Holy Spirit head-on.

So, let's get to it!

Inspect, Reflect, Apply

1. What have been some of the influences in your life that have helped your spiritual growth?

2. Have you had any experiences that made you want to know the Helper more? What might some of these be?

3. Have you had any experiences that made you want to turn away from the Helper? What did you do with those experiences?

Kinda Kooky

"Flight attendants, please take your seats immediately."

The captain came on the loudspeaker with an authority and urgency that made everyone sit up and take notice—most of all me. I'm not a relaxed traveler who can roll with the punches. A turbulent flight makes me feel like my nerves have been dipped in battery acid.

I especially hate flying on Halloween, as we were doing for this flight. People dress up in freaky costumes and think they're being playful, but it creeps me out.

Suffice it to say I was ready to jump out of my skin. And then there was the dressed-up mutant sitting next to me.

"Do you enjoy flying?" he asked, as though everything about this situation was normal.

"Flying is okay," I replied, trying to keep the talking to a minimum through my curt answer and by keeping my nose buried in my book.

"I love to travel," he said. "Particularly on Halloween—as you can see from my costume."

He was a young guy, maybe one of those artistic techie types, and was wearing an outfit that seemed to blend the emperor from *Star Wars* with Sauron, the traitor from *Lord of the Rings*. Definitely creepy.

"Where are you headed?" he asked.

I couldn't help thinking, *Why would you wear a costume like that and think someone would want to talk with you?*

But rather than being snarky, I said my friend had organized a surprise trip and we were flying to Chicago to see the musical *Wicked*.

"Me, too!" he said.

He was far too enthusiastic for my comfort level, and I was getting more and more creeped out by him, to say nothing of the ongoing turbulence. Unfortunately, the seat-belt sign was illuminated and I couldn't escape to the bathroom. I nudged Naomi and gave her a look, appealing for help.

Voila!

Naomi jumped into the conversation with the diplomacy and respect she wears like a coat of honor.

"Sir, tell me about your costume," she said, leaning past me. "I'm interested to hear how you came up with your idea."

You would have thought somebody flashed a green "talk now" signal. The guy took off on a long, detailed description of how he'd been planning this trip the last eighteen months and that the costume was the culminating component of his grand plan. Wearing it on the airplane provided him with a mock run-through to see how people would respond before he wore it to *Wicked*. I tuned him out after that, so I never learned the connection between his costume and the musical.

Naomi, on the other hand, listened with sincere interest.

When he stopped to come up for air, she said, "Hey, Ruth, let's switch seats. I know you prefer the window seat, and you can take a catnap, if you'd like."

That was music to my ears, and I happily complied, eager to let Naomi continue the interaction with Sauron the Jedi Emperor without me. My seat belt was off in a flash, and I pushed up the armrest so we could trade seats before he continued talking.

Once he saw he had a captive audience, Sauron became Jedi motormouth. And to my great relief, Naomi was now my shield from Mr. Creepy.

I closed my eyes, leaned my head against the window and tried to doze off, feeling safe and protected. It was difficult to sleep with the plane bouncing around, though. Just when I would be about to drop off, the plane would take a huge plunge and we'd be suspended in air for a nanosecond—more acid on my nerves. There would be no sleeping on this plane. But now that I'd been rescued by Naomi, it was enough for me to keep my eyes closed and rest my head against the window.

Naomi continued to occupy Sauron in conversation. Soon enough, the pilot came on the speaker to let us know we were starting our descent into Chicago, and he apologized for the turbulent ride. Sauron and Naomi talked all the way through the landing.

As Sauron was getting up to collect his luggage from the overhead bin, he paused and said, "Hey, why don't we meet up this weekend and talk some more? I've thoroughly enjoyed our conversation!"

He was like a Labrador puppy, full of enthusiasm, and I worried that he had translated Naomi's diplomacy for genuine interest—or worse, that she would consider his offer. Rather than answer without my input, though, she glanced over her shoulder at me, where she immediately saw on my face that I thought it was a *no bueno* idea.

"You are such a kind person to make that gracious offer," she said, turning back to him, "but we have a limited amount of time in Chicago, so I think we'll pass. Nevertheless, have a fabulous time in the Windy City, and best of luck with your costume fun!"

And that was the end of a potential catastrophe. I breathed a sigh of relief.

Once we caught a cab to take to our hotel, Naomi asked me about what happened.

"Are you doing okay?" she asked. "You seemed pretty stressed out on our flight. What was up?"

"For starters, I don't do well on bumpy flights. And the freaky costume guy gave me the creeps. The longer he tried to talk with me, the more uncomfortable I became. I'm not sure why."

"Well, he was pretty kooky," Naomi agreed. "As I talked with him, it became clear why you would have been more than a little creeped out. His costume was just the tip of the iceberg. He told me about his sad and twisted upbringing, along with some really violent things that were done to him in his childhood.

"I really wanted to help him with his struggles, but he seemed stuck in some paralyzing mindsets that have locked him in the kooky zone. It seems like he reverts into a fantasy world to keep from dealing with the overwhelming pain from his past."

"That is so sad for him," I replied.

"Yes, it is. My heart was breaking for him, and I wanted to help, but he wanted nothing of the sort. Anyway, I'm glad I could run interference for you so his kookiness didn't have to sidetrack you from enjoying our fun getaway."

The next thirty-six hours were a whirlwind of great fun and friendship. Every little bit of it, including the way Naomi handled things on the plane, made me even more grateful for my friend, kook filter extraordinaire.

4

Trick or Truth

There are two ways to be fooled. One is to believe what isn't true; the other is to refuse to believe what is true.

SØREN KIERKEGAARD

"The Spirit of truth, whom the world cannot receive, because it does not see Him or know Him, but you know Him because He abides with you and will be in you."

JOHN 14:17

I hate it when people lie to me, and I particularly hate it when my kids lie to me. I would rather have them tell me a gory and abysmal truth than have them tell a lie. In my mind, lying adds insult to injury. While I may not like hearing bad news, if a person lies to me on top of giving me bad news, the lying makes the bad news even worse.

The real problem, though, is when we lie to ourselves and believe our own propaganda. That is when we get into some bad trouble.

For example, when I was in high school, I wanted to be an amazing basketball player. It was my dream to play college basketball, so I practiced a lot, played in all the summer leagues that I could and even went to a college basketball camp in California with some of my friends. I loved basketball and had been committed to the sport for five years by the time I went to the camp in California.

But I got an abrupt reality check at this camp.

I was talking with one of the camp counselors, sharing with him my dream of playing college basketball, and he looked at me with kind eyes and told me in direct, clear and compassionate terms that this dream of mine would never happen.

I was aghast. He was not supposed to say that kind of thing—something that crushed my hopes and dreams. Nevertheless, he was forthright and explained that while I had a lot of passion and zeal for the sport, I did not have the talent required for the collegiate level of play.

His words to me were a helpful reality check. Up to that point, I had convinced myself I could play college ball because I wanted it bad enough and was committed to work as hard as I needed to get there. But I was self-deceived—and I preferred to live in my delusion.

Deception is no friend, regardless of the disguise, appeal or season. But it is easy to find people around us who suffer from it. Sometimes they do not even seem to suffer from the deception. This reminds me of a joke I once heard:

Doctor: Does your family suffer from mental illness?
Patient: Why, no, doctor. We quite enjoy our delusions!

We see evidence of deception in modern society, where it takes on many effective disguises. Take, for example, the television commercials that lead the viewers to believe they will become ultrahealthy if they buy a fitness gadget or program being advertised—oh, but do not forget you have to use it! Or the assumption we make that a person who dresses as a crisp, upscale professional has everything working out in their life. It can be easy to believe money is the equivalent of success and that poverty equals failure. In truth, success and failure, from God's perspective, is not defined by one's possessions or lack of possessions. If we are not careful, the allure of such deceptions can ensnare us.

Two Paths of Deception

There are two ways we might be deceived. One is internal, like with self-deception. The other is external, like when someone lies to you.

1. Internal

My story of wanting to be an amazing basketball player is a great example of self-deception. In truth, we are all vulnerable to this kind of deception. We so easily trick ourselves into believing what is not true.

Perhaps you can relate to some of these examples:

- Have you ever thought someone liked you romantically, only to discover they had no such interest in you?
- Have you ever thought you were not smart enough to pass a subject in school but, after giving some honest effort, discovered you had a hidden talent for the subject?
- Have you ever thought a group of people disliked you, only to discover they were distant or aloof because they respected you?
- Have you ever thought you were popular with a group, only to discover they were nothing more than back-stabbing sharks?
- Have you ever thought your opinion was more important in a situation than it really was?

I remember admiring one of my classmates in elementary school who lived just down the street. I thought she was way cool because she was athletic, took gymnastics lessons and had a trendy family. I thought we were buddies because we went to the same school, shared a similar interest in athletics and lived near each other. Imagine my disappointment when I realized she was not my friend and would not even sit with me on bus rides home from school.

Here is a more recent story. One time I was doing some baking and not paying close attention to the recipe or its ingredients because I was in a hurry. As a result, I used baking soda instead of baking powder. Big mistake. I did not realize I had made the mistake until we tasted, shall we say, a "textural discrepancy."

Because I thought the baking soda was something different than it was, that small deception wound up ruining my baking effort for the day. The integrity of the outcome was compromised by a small deception with the ingredients. That is something worth thinking about.

There are lots of ways we can be self-deceived, and no one seems immune from the problem. But the wake-up call that rouses us from the sleepy state of self-deception can be really awful—much worse than a batch of badly made baked goods.

For example, I once knew someone who had a seemingly happy marriage for several decades. She woke up one morning to find her husband standing by the bed with his suitcases packed. As she wiped the sleep from her eyes and tried to understand what was happening, he said, "Our marriage has been a sham for many years now, and I've decided to leave for greener pastures. Best of luck!"

Of course, there had been some telling signs of his dissatisfaction in the preceding years: extended business trips that included no explanation, a waning interest in their physical relationship and an emotional distance she had chalked up to the masculine profile. His departure was, indeed, a rude wake-up call. But she had allowed herself to be deceived into thinking everything was okay when it clearly was not.

Yes, we can mislead ourselves into half-baked illusions. Here is a poem I wrote to capture our tendency toward doing this without the Helper's help:

I Could Evaporate

Without You, I could evaporate
I could slip away into

63

Esoteric, ethereal and cloudy oblivion
Vaporous, detached and immaterial

But You keep my feet on the ground
Engaged in time and place
Connecting, attaching, shaping, present
You hold me here and now

Sometimes hostage, sometimes victim
Mostly intimate, consoling and encouraging
I think I'm watching and listening for You
And I know You are listening and watching me

Grounded, earthy, connecting, present
Although Spirit, more concrete than bonded atoms
Electrons and protons attracting, stabilizing
Neutral and attached

Without You, I could evaporate, dissipate and
    disappear

2. External

While internal deceptions can provide us with rude awakenings, external deceptions can be equally uncomfortable and disastrous. Take, for example, what happened between Eve and the snake in the Garden of Eden (see Genesis 3). Deception stood at the center of the dialogue that introduced sin to the human race. Even more central to this scenario was the voice of the one speaking through the snake—the original deceiver, Satan.

Jesus says that when the devil lies, he speaks his native language because he is the father of lies (see John 8:44). The devil's efforts to trick Eve were grounded in guile and deceit—fundamentally, in who the devil is. If Eve had known the serpent was deceiving her, I believe she would have made different choices. Nevertheless, she was deceived.

I believe the same is true for us today. If you are like me, you do not want to be tricked, deceived or duped. We may lie to ourselves willingly, but we do not want others to lie to us.

One time a person called me who acted like he knew me. But when he greeted me with my maiden name, which I had not used in more than twenty years, I smelled a rat. I tried to be friendly, asking, "Can you please help me remember how I know you?" His answer tied him to a long-ago friend from middle school, and I became even more suspicious. Then he proceeded to share experiences connected to the college I attended, and it became clear I had never met this person. He wanted me to contribute to a cause and was using information he knew about me to make it seem we were friends from yesteryear, when in actual truth, we had never met.

External deception can happen a number of ways, but when it is connected to a relationship, it is easy to get angry, bitter and distrustful in that relationship. Indeed, the absence of trust is often due to the presence of deception, which fosters detachment and undermines intimacy. These responses are never part of the recipe for staying connected or growing closer to someone, though.

In contrast, one reason our heavenly Father gives us the Spirit of truth is so we have an essential ingredient for growing in a trusting and ever-deepening relationship with God. Truth is an essential component of genuine and lasting intimacy, and it is at the core of our relationship with our heavenly Father through the Helper.

Two Names for the Holy Spirit

When Jesus first introduces the Holy Spirit to His disciples in John 14, He uses two names to describe Him. First, as we discussed in chapter 2, Jesus introduces the Holy Spirit as our Helper. Then, immediately on the heels of that name, Jesus offers a second—and strategic—name for the Holy Spirit: the Spirit of truth. He says, "The Spirit of truth, whom the world cannot receive, because it does not see Him or know Him, but you know Him because He abides with you and will be in you" (verse 17).

This naming of the Helper as the Spirit of truth is good news for all of us. As we have already made clear, truth is an essential but elusive quality in modern life. Consequently, this makes the Spirit of truth all the more important for our daily living.

When we think about the importance of truth, let's look into what the Greek word for *truth* in John 14:17 means. The word Jesus uses, *aletheia*, is the negative form of the words *hidden*, *overlooked* and *unaware*. If we take the opposite of each of these words, we learn a lot we can apply to our understanding of the Holy Spirit.

For starters, we find that the opposite of *unaware* is *aware*, the opposite of *overlooked* is *seen* and the opposite of *hidden* is *revealed*. This means the Holy Spirit, our Helper, is the Spirit of truth, who reveals, helps us see and makes us aware, removing obscurity and deception by virtue of who He is. The Spirit of truth provides:

- Illumination where there is darkness
- Clarity where there is obscurity
- Transparency where there is blurriness

- Awareness where there is ignorance
- Presence where there is absence

To me, this revelation of the Helper as the Spirit of truth is awesome because I know how vulnerable I can be to deception and distortion, both internally and externally. I find this characteristic of the Helper to be fantastic because, as I said above, truth is a fundamental component of intimacy. Inward truth and outward truth lay the groundwork for deep intimacy and connection. Indeed, without truth, we cannot be close to someone or have deep or lasting intimacy with them.

I know this from firsthand experience. When my husband, Reece, and I were first getting to know each other, I was teaching high school and coaching the girls' basketball team at a school in Denver, Colorado. Reece was living in Kansas City, and his parents had both died recently. I invited him to join our family for Thanksgiving as a getaway from some of the sadness that often accompanies the first holidays after a family member's death.

He spent a few days with our family and came to one of my basketball practices. My team was eager to find an opportunity to tease me about having a boyfriend, but I did not want to be teased, so I introduced him as a friend of my parents. He told me afterward that he did not feel we were bonding, and then he promptly flew back to Kansas City.

The honest truth was that I did not have the courage to let my basketball girls know I was romantically interested in him, and this hurt his feelings. He did not say it had hurt him, and I was dishonest about how I felt about him. As a result, we were both hurt, and it took some time and conversation for us to grow in greater transparency and vulnerability with each other.

The conversations that followed were foundational for us. They helped us be honest with each other, and they laid the groundwork for constructive communication. I would suggest that truth, in concert with genuine love, is the foundation for any constructive, healthy, close relationship.

I find that when I let the Holy Spirit speak truth into my life, my intimacy with the Holy Spirit grows deeper. While I have experienced this reality in my human relationships, like with my husband, I have found that truth is the essential bedrock of all the intimacy that grows in my relationship with the Helper, too.

Two Expressions of Deception

I described two pathways to deception above—the internal path and the external path—but there are many different expressions deception can take along these pathways. One of those expressions is pretending to be someone we are not. In 1 Samuel 17, we see that David was highly motivated to kill Goliath. King Saul was fine with David trying to kill the giant, but he asked David to wear his—the king's—armor, which was too big for David. No matter how hard David tried, Saul's armor would not fit him.

This is similar to what happens with deception. No matter how hard we try, especially when we are trying to be someone other than who we are, deception just does not work. It does not fit.

Being authentic and true to who God has made us to be is the best and safest journey for any deeper relationship we may have. I have found that attempting to change the interior Sarah—who I am—would be like putting goatskin on a giraffe and pretending the giraffe's neck is just an odd-shaped goat. Attempts to be someone we are not are futile, frustrating and confusing.

Another expression of deception happens when someone tries to fit us into a mold or a projection of who they are. I have had relationships with people who tried to connect with me as though I was someone I am not. For example, there were a few occasions growing up in Sunday school when I got into trouble for being mischievous. Sometimes the person correcting me would pull out the "pastor's kid should set a better example" lecture. Thankfully, that happened only a few times, as the lion's share of my teachers were beyond patient and gracious with me.

As I have aged, though, there have also been instances where people attempted to interact with me the same way they relate to my mom, as though we are a matched set and share a common identity. There was no future in that type of connection for me because it carried a fundamental absence of truth.

When all the dust settles, there is no one with whom you are more authentically yourself than the Spirit of truth. No one knows you better than the Holy Spirit, full stop. With the Holy Spirit, you live in complete truth.

Two Ways to Miss It

When Jesus says the world "cannot receive" the Spirit of truth (John 14:17), He contrasts His followers with nonfollowers based on how they relate to the Helper. He says nonfollowers do not have the ability to receive the Spirit of truth because they do "not see Him or know Him."

When Jesus says this—that the world "cannot receive" the Spirit of truth—He uses the Greek word *dunamis* (from which we derive our English word *dynamite*), and this word has a wide array of meanings. In this situation, it means "to lack the ability or power to do something." Consequently, it means those who do not follow Jesus lack the ability to receive the Helper. It is interesting to note, too, that *dunamis* is used in the Greek present tense in this verse, and in Greek, this tense means something having continuous action, rather than being a onetime event or occasion. When Jesus uses the present tense of this verb, it tells us their inability to receive truth is something that happens continuously.

Nonfollowers of Jesus lack the ability to receive the Helper, Jesus says, because they do not see or know the Helper. In Greek, a few words can be translated *see* in English—*blepo*, *orao* and *theoreo*—and Jesus chooses *theoreo*, which is a rich and substantial word in the Greek language. It is the derivative for our word *theater*, and it carries the idea of watching intently as a spectator or observing with concentration.

Jesus could have used the Greek word *blepo*, which refers to seeing with one's eyes or casting a quick glance, but that word does not carry the same level, intensity or connection as *theoreo* does. In short, Jesus is saying the people who do not follow Him lack the ability to receive the Spirit of truth because they do not pay close attention to the Helper.

Furthermore, Jesus says nonfollowers cannot receive the Spirit of truth because they do not know the Spirit of truth. This word *know*, in the Greek, is the word *ginosko*. It is a commonly used word throughout the New Testament and refers to knowledge a person gains from experience.

For example, I know (*ginosko*) how to snowboard because I have a lot of experience with this adventure. My experiences with snowboarding have taught me the importance of wearing a helmet, learning to balance on the edges of my snowboard and slowing down from time to time so I do not hit someone or get hurt. I know how to snowboard because of my experiences.

Applying this to the nonfollowers of Jesus, then, who lack the ability to receive the Helper, Jesus is saying this is because they have not learned from experience, insight or growth who the Helper is. Nonfollowers are at a significant disadvantage compared to followers because they are not paying attention to the Helper or learning about the Helper. This renders them unable to receive the Helper.

In contrast, followers of Jesus can receive the Spirit of truth because they intently look for and know the Helper through their various experiences.

Given this perspective, I become altogether challenged to get better and better at paying attention to and experiencing the Spirit of truth. Don't you? When we do this, we are able to receive the Helper.

Two Ways to Receive Help

As the verse in John 14:17 continues, Jesus contrasts His nonfollowers and followers yet again by saying the Spirit of truth "abides with" His followers and "will be in" them. The thing worth noticing here is the progression—a movement from having the Helper abide with us to having the Helper live inside us.

The Greek word for *abide* is *meno,* and it means "to live with or to dwell." Jesus uses this word quite extensively in John 15 when He offers the metaphor of the vine and branches, teaching His disciples to abide in the vine. But here Jesus increases the connection His followers will have with the Helper in the future, explaining that the Spirit of truth will not just abide with them but actually live inside them.

As a follower of Jesus, understanding that the Spirit of truth lives in me is comforting because there are times when my thinking goes rogue and I let myself get deceived. For example, I was recently on my way to meet an important person for lunch for the first time and was quite nervous about it. As I was driving to the lunch appointment, I could feel apprehension rummaging around in my thoughts, looking for me to join a party of insecurity.

When I found a parking spot near the lunch location, I took a deep breath and asked the Helper to help me. As I got out of the car, I was reminded of what Paul said in Romans 8:6—that the mind of the flesh is death but the mind set on the Spirit is life and peace. Walking the few blocks to the restaurant, I directed my attention to the part of the verse that talks about the mind being set on life and peace. I focused on life and peace instead of the stress, fear, insecurity and anxiety that threatened to creep in. When I arrived at the restaurant, I found the person I was to meet, and we had a fantastic time getting to know each other. The Helper empowered me with peace and life for that appointment, and I carried those things with me instead of my previously insecure jitters.

When I consider the Spirit of truth, I am encouraged that this Third Person of the Trinity is not some spooky, kooky, esoteric or misty idea that evaporates under stress, distortion or scrutiny. Rather, the Spirit of truth is integrated into my daily living, keeping me aligned with truth and protected from deception. As we learn how to walk in truth with the Helper, we will find ourselves less vulnerable to internal and external deception. The Holy Spirit is our beacon of truth in a deceptive world.

Inspect, Reflect, Apply

1. Consider a time in your past when you thought something was true, only to find out it was a startling deception. What was that like for you?

2. In what areas of your life are you most susceptible to deception?

3. Who or what could be some valuable truth indicators in your life? (Some possibilities might include a friend who is always honest with you, a weekly weigh-in appointment or a time log that helps you track how you spend time.)

4. In what ways, as a follower of Jesus, do you find yourself sensitive and attentive to truth?

5. In what ways do you find yourself repelled by deception, delusion and distortion?

Triqué

"High step—one, two, three! Again, high step—one, two, three!"

I had decided to try the new Zumba workout group at the rec center, and I was working my butt off—literally. I've always enjoyed exercise, even though I'm quite uncoordinated. That lack of coordination makes my workouts all the more entertaining. So trying out Zumba felt like catapulting into creative and comic chaos. So much fun!

One of the ladies I (literally) bumped into during the class was friendly, forgiving and gracious. I was particularly impressed with her poise, considering I knocked her to the ground by accident on one of the Zumba moves.

After collecting her wits, she popped up and said with a sincere smile, "Don't sweat it—we all make mistakes. You're doing great!"

When class was over, I learned her name was Triqué, taken from her French heritage.

"You seem so agile," I said to her. "How long have you been doing Zumba?"

"Well, I used to teach this class," she said, "but I had to take a break because of some health challenges. But you're doing extremely well for having joined only a few classes. I've been watching your progress—great job!"

Of course, despite her polite compliment, I was embarrassed.

After collecting my stuff, I bumped into Triqué again on the way out the door, and we agreed to meet up before the next class so she could give me a few pointers.

I told Naomi about the comic collision with Triqué, and she laughed with me and encouraged me to keep trying.

"The only way you get better at this stuff is to keep going," she said. "I'm so proud of you. Keep up the good work, Ruth, and have fun learning from Triqué."

With Naomi's encouragement and my determination serving as fuel, I met up with Triqué as planned. Imagine my surprise when she arrived limping with a cane, pale and languid—a radical departure from the vibrant and engaging Triqué I'd knocked down a few days earlier.

"What happened to you?" I asked, alarmed. "Were you in a car wreck?"

"Yes, and it was really bad," she said. "This guy T-boned me after running a stoplight. The police think he was driving over forty miles an hour when he slammed into me. I thought about not coming to meet you, but I didn't have your number or any way to let you know about my accident. I can give you a few pointers, but I need to get back to bed pretty quickly."

Triqué was in no shape to have a lengthy conversation, so she explained a few quick moves, watched me practice and then limped away after exchanging phone numbers. Needless to say, Zumba wasn't nearly as fun that day, as I was preoccupied with Triqué and concerned for her health.

Naomi called on my drive home from class, eager to hear about my exercise adventure.

"How was Zumba?" she asked. "Did you knock anyone down again? Did Triqué help you gain some coordination wisdom?"

It probably goes without saying that I love Naomi's affirming and encouraging spirit. It's one reason I'm so quick to pick up the phone when she calls.

"Today wasn't so whippy," I said. "Triqué was in a car wreck and badly injured, so class wasn't as much fun. I'm really concerned for her."

"That's awful! I'm so sorry to hear about her accident."

"Yeah, I'm pretty bummed out," I said. "And I was looking forward to having a new workout partner in Zumba. But now I'm not sure about her recovery. She's banged up bad."

"What can we do to help?" Naomi asked. "Does she need some meals? Someone to drive her to doctor appointments? Can we run errands—get her some groceries or pick up her kids from school?"

One of the other things I love about Naomi is how practical she is. While I can easily get quagmired in my passions and emotions, Naomi turns her affection into practical help. She jumps into the deep end with both feet and hands to give help, often changing everything in miraculous ways. I could tell in that moment she was doing her creative thinking, so I was eager to join the adventure that I knew would be filled with unexpected twists.

"Wow," I said. "I love how practical you are! I was stuck in the place of feeling Triqué's pain, but you used those feelings and turned them into something constructive—that's awesome! I'll text her right now and ask how we can help."

I shot a brief text to Triqué, and she replied quickly with an essential grocery list, so Naomi and I met back at the grocery store where our friendship first started. After collecting the few items and getting Triqué's home address, we hopped in the car and made our way there.

As we walked up to the house, I felt Naomi go into hypervigilant mode. It was like her nerves came out of her skin, exposed to every fleeting sniff, whiff and imperceptible shift. I could tell she was growing increasingly uncomfortable with each step we took closer to Triqué's home. She even said, "I smell a rat."

Of course, I thought she meant a literal rotting mouse. I don't have near the level of perception or sensitivity she does.

I rang the doorbell, groceries in hand, and Triqué opened the door and stood there looking coy, cunning and, well, tricksy.

I was taken off guard. She appeared altogether different from the frail and pale Triqué I'd encountered at the rec center a short while ago. This Triqué looked healthy, robust and agile.

I could tell Naomi was taken by surprise, too, having expected to see a debilitated person but instead being greeted by someone who looked to be the epitome of health.

"Welcome to my house," Triqué said. "Come in, and let me help with the groceries. As you can see, I feel really great—a miraculous recovery!"

I made a quick introduction of Naomi to Triqué, and Naomi's response could not have been more chilly or detached. I had never felt more awkward in my life.

"Please come in and make yourselves at home," Triqué said. "The kitchen is back this way. Let me make you some hot tea to help you get comfortable. I'm sure you're curious to hear how I've recovered in such a few short hours!"

She clearly planned for us to stay awhile, but I knew Naomi wanted nothing of the sort when she said, "We won't be staying but for a minute to drop off the groceries, so please don't trouble yourself with making tea."

I felt caught in the middle of some weird vibes and strange energy. It was like Triqué was trying to taint the air with elusive deceptions and Naomi was shattering the poisoned air with sharp absolutes. I didn't want to be rude to my new friend with the drop-and-dash grocery errand, but I also didn't want to blow off Naomi, whom I'd grown to enjoy and trust.

Nevertheless, I thought the least we could do would be to listen to Triqué's explanation of her miracle recovery.

"Thanks so much for your gracious offer to have us stay," I said. "We'd be happy to stay for just a few minutes and hear your amazing story—but let's skip the tea."

"This chick is a fake, and she's playing you," Naomi muttered.

Even though I heard Naomi's words, I was curious to hear Triqué's explanation.

"Well, I was in tremendous pain when you saw me this morning," Triqué began as she led us into her kitchen, "and I wasn't able to explain much, so thanks for helping with my groceries. After I met up with you at the gym, I came home and drank an elixir—kind of a potion concoction—that I found off the Internet. And look at me now—that stuff is miraculous!"

I could feel Naomi was about to jump out of her skin and that she was doing everything in her power to stay there and not bolt out the front door.

With grace and supernatural poise, she said, "Wow, Triqué, I've only just met you in the last few minutes, and your story sounds unbelievable—with a heavy emphasis on the *un* part of *believable*."

Triqué squared her shoulders and turned toward me. "Ruth, I see your friend is quite skeptical about my miraculous recovery. Please help me convince her I was sick and now I'm well."

What an awful turn of events! I hated being squished in the middle with deception, smoke and mirrors dancing in the air. For me, this seemed a no-win situation—that is, until Naomi chimed in.

"Triqué, there's no need to force Ruth to defend and align with you," my dear friend said. "Please show us your car that was wrecked."

"Who do you think I am?" Triqué asked, jumping from her seat with her eyes flashing. "Are you calling me a liar? Ruth, what kind of person are you bringing into my home?"

The friendly, bubbly, outgoing Zumba buddy I'd recently met had transformed into a venomous, accusatory and harsh imposter. I was speechless!

"Ruth, please don't feel like you're caught in the middle of this conflict," Naomi said in her ever-calm voice. "I'm more than happy to let you stay and enjoy some tea with Triqué. I can come back and give you a ride home at any time that would suit you. If you'd prefer to come with me now, we can leave the groceries for Triqué and step away from this tricky situation—no pun intended."

I was struggling with this unforeseen clash and stopped for a second to collect my thoughts. I remembered Triqué seemed almost too nice when I knocked her down in Zumba. Bumping into her on the way out the door that same day seemed almost preplanned. The more I thought about it, the more smoky everything became.

Finally, I remembered Naomi's words as we walked up to Triqué's house: "I smell a rat."

I turned to Triqué. "It's probably time for us to leave," I said. "I don't think I can understand what you're doing or saying without getting hurt or tricked in the process. Thanks for your recent help in Zumba, and I wish you the best of luck for your future."

With those words, Naomi and I turned and walked out the front door, and Triqué closed the door after us.

We walked toward the car, and Naomi said, "Ruth, one of the things I really love about you is your willingness to meet new people and embrace them as friends. But sometimes that can be a tricky path because not everyone is as they appear on the surface. Truth will keep you out of the weeds of deception. It will keep your relationships and heart pure for the best and safest friendships. Let's always agree to keep truth as a premium value in our friendship."

"Thanks, Naomi," I said. "I appreciate your wisdom and insight. Truth establishes trust, and trust is built on time and honesty. Thanks for being truthful and trustworthy, my friend."

On that clean and authentic note, I hopped in Naomi's car and we worked out a time to grab coffee later that week.

5

The Flawless Parent

A man is but the product of his thoughts. What he thinks, he becomes.

MAHATMA GANDHI

"I will not leave you as orphans; I will come to you."

JOHN 14:18

I recall with vivid agony being in Beirut, Lebanon, when I was five years old and getting locked in a bathroom on the second floor of a restaurant where our group was eating. My parents were leading a Holy Land tour and had brought my brother and me on this trip of a lifetime. I had enjoyed the trip. Seeing new sights, being in the places where biblical events had occurred and experiencing the Bible coming alive to me in 3-D—this was all powerful stuff for a five-year-old.

But the bathroom in Beirut was not good in any way.

It was evening. After a long day of travel and touring, everyone was eating dinner. I asked permission to use the restroom, which was difficult to find by myself. Upon finishing my business, I went to unlock the door, but it would not open.

After repeated attempts, I started to panic and began screaming for someone to come and let me out. The bathroom was not the kind where you could crawl under the stall and get out. But there was a window over the toilet. I thought maybe I could climb through the window and jump down, since we were on the second floor.

When I looked out the window to see how far down it was to the ground, I saw a soldier with a machine gun looking up at me. This freaked out my five-year-old brain and emotions!

The seconds seemed to pass slowly, and when I found no one was coming to get me, I started to think my parents were going to leave me there and I would be stuck in Beirut, Lebanon—wherever that was—forever.

I began banging on the door and yelling as loud as I could, hoping someone would come and let me out. After what seemed to be an eternity, my brother and mother showed up, helped me get out and endeavored to calm me down. The experience still makes me feel jittery and panicky today.

Are You an Orphan?

There is a good chance you had an experience in your childhood that made you feel abandoned. Maybe a best friend moved away and you missed them terribly. Maybe your parents got divorced and there were moments you felt one of them had left you. As an adult, maybe you have experienced a similar sense of abandonment. Perhaps a spouse left you for a military responsibility, a temporary job assignment or another relationship.

Feeling abandoned is awful, and we do all kinds of things to help ourselves feel better and recover from these kinds of experiences. But frequently, they leave a mark on our souls. And if we do not get help to sort them out, that feeling of being abandoned can become a difficult obstacle to manage and resolve. It can grow into something worse than the original experience.

Here is the thing: Abandonment can develop an orphan mindset in us. In the passage we have been exploring in John 14, Jesus confronts this orphan mindset by sharing the way the Helper immunizes us from its destructive effects. He says, "I will not leave you as orphans; I will come to you" (John 14:18).

It was necessary for Jesus to discuss this with His disciples in light of what they were about to experience: His arrest, crucifixion, resurrection and ascension. They would likely feel abandoned by those events—after all, they had been with Him every day for three continuous years, and suddenly He would be gone. Such feelings of abandonment could lead them to an orphan mentality, and He wanted to prevent that from happening.

To understand the weight of what Jesus communicates here, let's back up a minute. Remember that in this John 14 passage, Jesus begins by saying the Holy Spirit is a Helper who will "be with you forever" (verse 16). For someone who has felt abandoned, imagine what that would be like to hear. Instead of abandonment being the order of the day, you learn you have someone with you for all time.

Consider, too, that when John wrote his gospel, he did not use punctuation, and he did not write the chapter and verse markers for us. Those are inventions of our modern, educated world. When John wrote, he did so with a continuous flow.

Bearing that in mind, let's reread the full passage we have studied so far:

> "I will ask the Father, and He will give you another Helper, that He may be with you forever; that is the Spirit of truth, whom the world cannot receive, because it does not see Him or know Him, but you know Him because He abides with you and will be in you.
>
> "I will not leave you as orphans; I will come to you."
>
> John 14:16–18

In Greek, a few indicators in the text are often used to denote a new thought or a pause in the text. None of those indicators were used by John between verse 17 and verse 18, so we can safely say Jesus' words flow continuously from verse 16 to the end of the quoted passage. This means we are meant to read the verses as a whole unit of thought rather than choppy compartments.

From these verses, then, we see that the Helper is:

- Part of the Trinity
- Helper
- Present with us everywhere
- Present with us all the time

- Spirit of truth
- Abiding
- Living in

As we look at this list describing who the Helper is, we find a correlation between who the Holy Spirit is and what an orphan thinks and feels.

What would it feel like to be an orphan? Many studies have been done about orphans, and a plethora of clinical observations and conclusions have been reached from such studies, but they are communicated in such a detached and sterile way. When I did some looking around, I came across the story of a person who grew up an orphan. This was their description of it:

> Most orphans would say that they want more than anything else to be rich and rise up in the world. So at least they could get away from being an orphan. Finding their birth parents is not that important to them though it may be a second choice. They know that their parents will never look for them.
>
> Being an orphan is not the way you want to live. When I was growing up, an orphan was second class. Some people thought orphans were "no good." It was lonely, painful, fearful. I worried about starvation. And people take advantage of orphans.
>
> After I got out of the orphanage, I was desperate. At the age of 17, I was completely by myself. I couldn't go back to the orphanage. But no one cared about me and what I was doing.[1]

Additionally, as I have observed orphans around the world through my humanitarian work with Saving Moses, I have come to understand that to-be-expected behavior and feelings for an orphan include isolation, apathy, defensiveness, perceiving themselves to be without comfort, a lack of sensitivity, independence, distrustfulness, vulnerability, fearfulness and helplessness. Furthermore, orphans often struggle to form healthy relational attachments.

While many of us may not be outright orphans, we can nonetheless relate to these orphan experiences of being abandoned, neglected, cast aside or rejected. When we are honest, we will say that we do not always manage those feelings or realities well and that we use coping techniques. Sometimes we try to compensate for a perceived shortcoming. Sometimes we withdraw so that it is more difficult to be rejected again. Sometimes we resort to unhealthy behaviors to try to fix the hurt, pain and emptiness we feel. These behaviors might include addictions, staying busy, unhealthy eating habits, extreme exercise, becoming hyper-religious or entering into unhealthy relationships.

The most helpful way to resolve this struggle is to remember what Paul teaches about the Helper—that having the Holy Spirit makes us adopted children. He says:

> For all who are being led by the Spirit of God, these are sons of God. For you have not received a spirit of slavery leading to fear again, but you have received a spirit of adoption as sons by which we cry out, "Abba! Father!" The Spirit Himself testifies with our spirit that we are children of God.
>
> Romans 8:14–16

For a person who feels abandoned or is an orphan, the Helper is the exact solution needed. Let's consider this contrast:

Orphan Experience	Helper's Offering
Alone and abandoned	Omnipresent and omnitemporal
Without comfort	Comfort
Independent	Abiding with
Isolated	Indwelling
Helpless	Help
Fearful and vulnerable	Truth to dispel deception and fear
Lack of trust in relationships	An experience of seeing and knowing

As we integrate our experience of the Helper into our daily living, we need to be aware of those times, seasons and situations where we have felt abandoned. We need to consider how those experiences developed an orphan mindset in us.

I came to realize the Beirut bathroom incident influenced me more than I realized, and its influence came to light as I began to pray and work through what Jesus teaches us about the Helper in this passage. I began to think about how abandoned I felt in that bathroom and the panic it created. Then I thought about other times in my life when I felt abandoned and had a similar reaction of panic. As I looked back on my life, I could see destructive behaviors that were rooted in the deception that I was alone and abandoned. Studying this verse helped unravel that deception and change my behavior in situations where I might have felt left out, abandoned or similar to an orphan. While I know I have not fully arrived on this, I am better at handling it than I was in the past, thanks to the Helper.

While it is one thing to deal with thoughts of abandonment, it is yet another thing to face its challenges in relationships. The Holy Spirit has helped me understand that healthy relationships start with having a healthy and integrated relationship with the Helper. The more access I give the Helper to my life—my thoughts, emotions, reflections, priorities, relationships and values—the more I behave as a whole person, rather than someone who is fragmented and orphaned.

What Is the Next Step?

Another time when I was young, a babysitter was supposed to meet me at my bus stop after school to bring me home. But there was a communication mix-up, and when the bus dropped me off, no one was there to collect me. As the bus drove away, I stayed at the bus stop, thinking someone would be along shortly and was probably just running late.

The longer I waited, the more nervous I became. Finally, after what seemed like an eternity (because time passes slowly when you are five), I started to think about what I should do next. I remember asking God to help me.

Then, even though I was in kindergarten, I started to think about my options. I could stay where I was and hope someone would come. I could knock on someone's door in the apartment building next to the bus stop and ask for help from a stranger. (That option did not seem good.) Or I could try to walk home and wait there.

I decided to walk home, as I felt a little bit more peace around that choice. Although my bus stop was not far from my house—just a few blocks, really—the journey was intimidating and scary.

I remember asking the Helper to be with me and help me along the way—to guide my steps, to direct my decisions, to protect me and keep me safe. I walked along and talked with the Helper the whole way, getting directions and guidance for little pieces of the journey at a time.

I walked the first block and came to the hill and canal behind our house. *Next step,* climb the hill. At the top, I could look across the canal and see our backyard and house, but I knew the canal, once I got to it, might be filled with water. *Next step,* navigate down the hill to check out the water level. There was a little water, but it was not too bad. I stood along the canal edge and asked the Helper to direct my steps across the canal, from rock to rock, until I got to the other side. *Next step,* climb the bank, maneuver through the thick foliage and head to the gate in our fence across the backyard.

I went through the gate and came to the back door of our house, only to discover the house was locked up. Front door, back door, side door, windows—everything was shut tight. But I waited with some relief on the back porch, feeling safe and glad to be at my house and not at the bus stop anymore.

Then I remembered my parents had one of those hidden key boxes. *Next step,* find the secret box. Thankfully, there was a key in it. I used it to open the back door and, with tremendous gratitude, walked into my house.

I remember breathing a deep sigh of relief and then wondering how to contact my parents to let them know I was home by myself but safe. I eventually learned the lady who was supposed to collect me from the bus stop had her times mixed up. She felt awful for not being there to pick me up. My parents were upset about what happened, too, but more than anything, they were glad I was safe.

As an adult, it would be easy to look back on that experience and dismiss it as "just one of those things" that happened in my childhood. However, doing so would mean missing the valuable lessons it holds. Through the literal journey I took that day, the Helper was with me at every step. He helped me with each decision. He helped me overcome obstacles. He calmed my fears. He attended to, guided, comforted, protected and engaged with me through the whole experience. So many takeaways from that one experience! They are lessons that teach me still today.

We may not take a literal journey like that today. However, the movement away from the orphan mindset is a journey in itself, and it is one that can seem overwhelming and insurmountable. In this, too, the Helper is here to walk alongside us, guiding us one step at a time. We may not know all the steps. We may not have a map. But the first step is to ask the Helper to help us and then to move forward, one step at a time.

What about Your Parents?

None of our earthly parents who raised us were without mistakes, deficiencies or foibles. Despite their best efforts, most compassionate motives or natural parenting instincts, they did not raise us perfectly. So, what do we do with that reality?

When I had my first child, I remember feeling overwhelmed with the gravity of being a parent. I wanted nothing more than to be the perfect mom for my daughter, but within 48 hours, I had already made mistakes. I remember thinking, *Wow! That whole "three strikes and you're out" concept doesn't apply to parenting. I've already messed up more than three times, and it hasn't even been a week.* I concluded there is no such thing as the perfect parent. All I could give was my best effort.

We often acknowledge our parents were flawed, and sometimes they get too much of the blame for our choices and dysfunctions. But we also fail to move beyond that initial acknowledgment much of the time. Maybe this is because we do not know where to go from there or because such acknowledgment is painful. I think as followers of Jesus, we also have the best of intentions and get queasy when identifying and wrestling with our parents' humanity because we do not want to dishonor them.

The truth is, if we are going to live out the destiny for which God created us, we must acknowledge the shortcomings of our parents and how those deficiencies affected us in both small and big ways. By stepping up to these realities, we invite the Helper—again, the Spirit of truth—to speak into our lives and bring about our transformation.

The Helper does not allow us to remain in the quagmire of human shortfalls, rejection, emptiness or debilitating pain. He does not leave us in the orphan mindset. Indeed, the only way out of such a quagmire is to snuggle up to the Helper, ask Him for help and follow Him along the journey of truth, one step at a time. It is a path that includes surrender, redemption and transformation.

Whether you had the best parents, the worst parents or no parents at all, the reality is that the Helper wants to come alongside you and be your perfect parent. Embracing this does not dishonor your earthly parents.

Let's talk about gender here, too. As I was preparing to write this book, I came across an interesting story in Catherine Marshall's book *The Helper*. In it, she describes how her husband, Peter, woke up early in the morning one day with severe chest pains and was rushed to the hospital in an ambulance. Later, he died from a heart attack. But in her state of alarm and panic, Catherine writes, "My knees no sooner touched the floor than I experienced God as a comforting Mother—something altogether new to me."[2]

The Helper, as the Holy Spirit, is not confined to a specific gender, as we are in our human experience. Rather, the Helper is able to interact with us in both a fatherly way, with strength and courage, as well as in a motherly way, with nurture and compassion.

The following verses may help you replace the orphan identity lurking in the shadows of your soul. Might I suggest you pick a few to memorize?

Upon You I was cast from birth; You have been my God from my mother's womb.

Psalm 22:10

"Can a woman forget her nursing child and have no compassion on the son of her womb? Even these may forget, but I will not forget you. Behold, I have inscribed you on the palms of My hands."

Isaiah 49:15–16

"As one whom his mother comforts, so I will comfort you."

Isaiah 66:13

The Spirit Himself testifies with our spirit that we are children of God.

Romans 8:16

Because you are sons, God has sent forth the Spirit of His Son into our hearts, crying, "Abba! Father!"

Galatians 4:6

"I will never desert you, nor will I ever forsake you."

Hebrews 13:5

See how great a love the Father has bestowed on us, that we would be called children of God; and such we are.

1 John 3:1

Will You Trust?

When we struggle with abandonment and have developed an orphan mindset, the problem of trust is a steady challenge. Trust can be a dicey topic even in the best of circumstances, to say nothing of what happens when we have been rejected or abandoned.

Trust is something with which almost everyone struggles. Perhaps you can recall a friendship or relationship that made you feel betrayed—maybe an unkept confidence, a moment of miscommunication or a difference in sensitivity. Whether we realize we are doing it or not, we often withdraw our trust when we feel betrayed. We also grade how much we trust someone based on what happens when we trust them with something important to us.

In the same way, we tend to trust God based on the outcomes of our prayers. If we get our prayers answered in the way we want, we trust God more. If God does not answer our prayers, we trust God less—and maybe we pray less, too.

If we base our trust in the Helper on outcomes, then we turn our relationship into one that is based on transactional intimacy: *If I get my way, then I'll stay close to You. If You don't do what I want, then I'll create space and distance from You.* This filter for trusting the Helper is a dead end because God is sovereign and omnipotent, not our personal puppet.

Is there a different premise on which to base our trust in the Helper? Let me suggest that we ground our trust on the character of the Helper rather than the outcomes of prayer. If you think about it, our deepest relationships are not grounded in what a person does but in who a person is. In a similar way, knowing who the Helper is fosters a greater trust in us and a deeper intimacy in the relationship.

Consider what it says in Proverbs 22:19 related to developing a greater level of trust in God: "So that your trust may be in the LORD, I have taught you today, even you." Perhaps we go through some of our challenges so we can learn to trust the Helper more. Our struggles can help us experience the Helper with greater power, clarity and connection—kind of like a school of lifelong learning.

As we finish out this chapter on the note of trusting God's character, let me remind you of Paul's words in Romans:

In the same way the Spirit also helps our weakness; for we do not know how to pray as we should, but the Spirit Himself intercedes for us with groanings too deep for words; and He who searches the hearts knows what the mind of the Spirit is, because He intercedes for the saints according to the will of God.

And we know that God causes all things to work together for good to those who love God, to those who are called according to His purpose.

Romans 8:26–28

We see from these verses that the Helper is an intercessor and endeavors to help us in our weaknesses. Furthermore, Paul helps us understand that the Helper prays for us in accordance with God's will. It is in the Helper's central identity to help us, to be continually present to us and to connect us in loving fellowship with our heavenly Father. The Helper offers us the assurance that we are not orphans. Indeed, the Helper wants to transform our actions and attitudes away from that erroneous belief and toward the truth that we are God's children, wholly loved.

Inspect, Reflect, Apply

1. Describe a time in your life when you felt abandoned.

2. Which parent—your mom or your dad—was the more difficult relationship for you when you were growing up, and why?

3. In what ways could the Helper help you resolve the difficulties you experienced with that parent?

4. What behaviors in your life provide evidence of an orphan mindset at work in you?

5. Where have you placed your trust in the past?

6. Ask the Helper to give you the strength to switch your trust to Him in little and big ways.

7. The Bible makes it clear we must honor our parents. This is non-negotiable. At the same time, it is important to be honest about who our parents have been for us and who they have not been for us. The following exercise will help strengthen your ability to hold this tension of bestowing honor but being honest. You are invited to consider people in the Bible who were parents and human in every way. Read the passage listed for each story, and then identify the ways honesty and honor could exist in each one.

The Parable of the Prodigal Son: Luke 15:11–32

Honest	Honor

Abraham and Isaac: Genesis 22:1–19

Honest	Honor

Jacob and his sons: Genesis 37:1–11; 45:25–28; 46:28–47:12

Honest	Honor

David, Amnon, Tamar and Absalom: 2 Samuel 13–18

Honest	Honor

Moses' mom: Exodus 2:1–10

Honest	Honor

Hannah and Samuel: 1 Samuel 1–2:10

Honest	Honor

Mary and Jesus: Luke 1:26–56; 2:1–51; John 2:1–5; 19:26–27

Honest	Honor

Crisis!

Over the siren noise, I yelled into my phone, "Can you come to the ER right away? My mom fell, and I think it's really serious."

I had called Naomi from the ambulance as we were rushing to the hospital. My mom had been with our family on a gentle hike through some nice trees that afternoon. We were glad to have her with us for some fresh air and sunshine.

My kids had run ahead, around the bend of the trail, when my mom twisted her ankle, fell and hit her head on a boulder next to the path. Immediately, she began to shake and her body became stiff.

"Catch up to the kids," I told my husband. "Keep them up there, and I'll call you in a minute."

I knew I wouldn't have the capacity to be with my mom while the kids freaked out to find her splayed on the park trail, her body shaking.

"Okay," he said. "But I told you it was a bad idea to bring your mom on this hike."

It was true. My mom hadn't been the epitome of good health, exercise or proper eating. She had her share of medical challenges, and they'd been a part of her life for as long as I could remember.

After trying to wake her to no avail, I called Pete on his cell.

"She's not responding," I said. "What should I do?"

"Is she breathing? Are her eyes open? Did you check her pulse?"

These questions forced me out of my emotional panic and into more focused attention on my mom's condition.

"Yes, she's breathing, and her eyes are open," I said, "but they're really glazed over and unfocused."

I reached for her wrist.

"I can feel her pulse, but it feels weak."

"Ruth, I'll stay with the kids and keep them settled. Call 911 and get your mom an ambulance. You need to get her to the hospital as soon as possible."

I hung up and called 911, then called Naomi from the ambulance.

When we arrived at the hospital, the medical staff rushed my mom into a curtained room. I followed and saw Naomi standing to the side, like she'd been at the hospital all along and was ready to help. She stood next to me, listening, as I answered questions from the medical staff.

"She was taking a trail walk with my family when she twisted her ankle," I told them. "She fell and hit her head on a boulder alongside the path. Then she started to shake. Her eyes became fixed, and she became unresponsive."

"Can you give us some of her medical background?" one of the nurses asked. "Does she have a history of diabetes, heart problems, any breathing conditions?"

These questions jogged my childhood memories, and while I tried to be helpful relaying her medical information, my emotions started to get the better of me. My eyes teared up, and my voice quivered.

"She has a mild case of a rare medical condition called Stone Man Syndrome," I said.

The nurse hadn't heard of the disorder, so I explained it was a condition where a person's soft tissues and joints harden and turn into bones.

As I was talking, Naomi put her hand on my shoulder. I immediately felt strength and comfort.

I remember going with my mom to multiple doctor appointments when I was really small, when she was still trying to figure out what her sickness was. Doctor after doctor and specialist after specialist—everyone was baffled by her symptoms, all of which I could describe with razor-sharp accuracy by the time I was six years old.

Then a sage specialist diagnosed her correctly. Prior to the diagnosis, my mom had endured all kinds of treatments that attempted to loosen her joints and soft tissue, which were always in pain despite a plethora of painkiller prescriptions. One doctor even said her condition was psychosomatic, which sent my mom into a depressive funk for several months.

But here was the real rub for me as a kid living through these ups and downs with my mom. Even though my intelligent mom had a strong personality and her character was nothing less than sterling, she was frequently preoccupied with her pain and stressed by the unsuccessful attempts to relieve and cure her ailments. This meant there weren't a lot of her emotions left over to connect with me as I grew up. I would often find myself in hyperindependent mode, and sometimes it was difficult for me to connect with others in sustained and meaningful friendships.

"Ruth, let's take a break and get a cup of coffee."

Naomi's words jolted me out of these memories of the past and back into the current reality: answering questions in the hospital ER to take care of my mom.

"Your mom is resting comfortably right now, and her vital signs are strong and stable," the nurse said. "We can call you if anything changes while you get a cup of coffee—that's no problem."

I was shaking on the inside as I walked down the hallway with Naomi, but I felt her comfort and strength radiating toward me with nurture and power.

"Go sit down and I'll bring you some decaf," she said when we reached the cafeteria.

Naomi always seemed to know exactly what I needed and when.

After she brought me the coffee, she sat down next to me and I fell apart. Tears flowed from my eyes, and I felt the emotional weight of being strong and independent all of my life. I couldn't hold that weight a moment longer.

Thankfully, Naomi was right there to ease that weight from my care. I buried my head in her shoulder, weeping and letting the grief, hurt, brokenness and dull fatigue wash out of me.

After some time, I said, "I think we should go back and check on Mom."

"Do you feel strong enough to do that?" she asked. "Or are you playing the role of the dutiful and supportive daughter?"

I paused and thought about her question. I wanted to be the dutiful and supportive daughter, because that was the natural role for me to play. But Naomi's question about feeling strong enough gave me pause.

Additionally, I noticed her question made me feel a bit closer to her—and as I drew closer, I began to feel stronger, safer, more healthy and resilient.

I cleared my throat. "Yes, I think I'm okay to go back now. I can't thank you enough, Naomi, for being here, for helping me, and for being so supportive, consoling and strong."

"No problem!" she said. "This is totally natural for me, and I love getting to be with you in this emergency. Thank you for calling me and letting me be here."

When we returned to my mom's curtained room in the ER, I looked at her face and could see her condition had worsened. She was pale.

The nurse said, "Perfect timing—I'm glad you're here because I was just going to call you. Your mom has taken a turn for the worse, and her vital signs are weakening."

"Why is that?" I asked. "What happened?"

"I'm not certain. Sometimes elderly people come into the ER with a simple malady and their condition rapidly deteriorates. I'm keeping a close watch on her. In the meantime, just because of her age, I have to ask if she has a DNR order in her legal paperwork."

What a wakeup call that was! Imagine your day going from a nice, sunny trail walk to being asked if your mom has a legal order not to resuscitate her.

Slowly, I replied, "Yes, a few years ago she organized her legal documents, her will and her medical preferences, and she gave me a copy. I recall seeing her DNR order."

When I'd asked my mom about it at the time, she explained that she'd lived a fulfilling life and had no interest in putting off what is ultimately inevitable.

Thankfully, Naomi was sitting next to me because I was starting to feel nauseous. I almost started to gag, in fact, but Naomi put her hand on my shoulder, immediately diverting my attention to her strength, comfort and reassurance.

"Okay, Ruth," explained the nurse. "Please understand that if your mom's condition continues to decline, her DNR order has already mandated our course of care, so you might want to think about what this could mean."

"Let's go call your husband," Naomi said.

I so appreciate Naomi's way of being practical and supportive at the same time.

I looked back at my mom. Her eyes were closed, and she looked comfortable and peaceful.

We stepped into the ER waiting room, and I called Pete.

"The nurse let me know that Mom's vital signs are declining," I told him, "and the nurse asked me if she has a DNR order."

There was a long pause on the other end, and I could feel him take a deep breath. I knew him well enough to know he was collecting his thoughts and carefully weighing what to say next.

Finally, he said, "Do you want me to come and bring the kids? Tell me how I can be supportive."

"Naomi is here with me," I said, "and while I'd love to have you here, too, someone needs to stay with the kids. I don't think it would be good for them to see her. She looks pale, weak and hollow. If I had to make a decision at this moment, I'd prefer to have their last memory of her be more pleasant than how she looks now."

"I understand," he said. "I'll do whatever I can to help you. And I'm glad Naomi is with you."

I was, too. And I felt relieved that Pete and the kids were okay.

Now I was faced with the daunting reality that my mom was dying and the final moments of her physical life were ebbing into eternity. Even though I was fully confident that I'd see my mom on the other side, the immediate reality of losing her was painful.

Naomi could tell I was teetering on the brink again, and she came over and held me close, infusing me with comfort, strength and support. I lingered in that hug for some moments, breathing in her fortitude and help.

Then we went back to Mom's bed. I looked at the monitors and could see her heart rate was decreasing and her blood pressure was declining. I was torn between wanting her to stay with me and wanting her to be free from the pain and struggle of managing the rare condition she'd endured the majority of her life.

In the end, I'm not sure how or when my mom passed because she just slipped away, all while Naomi was sitting close to me and offering me nothing less than continual comfort and sustenance.

As I write this now, five years after my mom's passing, I still feel the occasional twangs of loss and grief, the unfriendly twins who remind us of our frail mortality. But my friendship with Naomi has also stepped into those places of loss. This friendship has even stepped into the childhood emotions that were broken and dysfunctional. Our friendship continues to fill in gaps, heal many scars and transform unseen dysfunction into glorious strength. While I've lost my mom, I've gained a deeper connection with Naomi, and for that I'm thankful.

6

Remember to Learn

The mind is not a vessel that needs filling, but
wood that needs igniting.

PLUTARCH

"But the Helper, the Holy Spirit, whom the Father will send in My name, He will teach you all
things, and bring to your remembrance all that
I said to you."

JOHN 14:26

My first experience of teaching was the ride of a lifetime. I
had just finished my junior year of college, having endured
a rather rigorous year learning German phonetics, literature,
language and grammar. My plan for the summer was to

continue studying German at a language school in south-west Germany.

However, I had about three weeks at home before my summer program began. I am not a person who can just take a three-week pause, so I was trying to figure out what to do with the time—maybe something that would let me earn a little money, which could help my college budget.

I learned of a three-week opening to be a substitute teacher for high school social studies at the school connected to my church in Denver. I was asked if I would be interested in the temporary position. Being more than a little impulsive and the type of person who leaps then looks, I said a quick yes and did not give it much thought. I figured I could land on my feet and handle anything for three weeks.

Once I finished a quick interview and the principal introduced me to the school and the subjects I would teach, I began to think about what I had gotten myself into. I remembered some of my high school mischief and chicanery, particularly when it came to substitute teachers. I recalled one poor guy who was a student teacher in my senior Bible class. He was supposed to be teaching us the book of Revelation. I gave him such a hard time that I think he reconsidered the whole teaching thing and pursued an alternative degree plan.

Now the shoe was on the other foot.

Being a substitute high school teacher for the last three weeks of a school year would not be an optimum setup. But even under these unfavorable conditions, I discovered I loved it. I loved my students, the rigor, the content and the energy I got from it. I even loved pretending I was an adult with a real job for three weeks.

Fast-forward six months, and I finished my degree a semester early. When I learned of an open position back at the same school, this time teaching social studies, PE and whatever else they needed for grades 6–12, I jumped at the chance and began my teaching career in January.

Yes, I entered my teaching career kind of topsy-turvy, but I quickly discovered the work fueled me. I felt like a fish in water and had discovered one of my God-given talents. I taught at the school for more than three years, and over the course of more than 25 years now, I have taught in various configurations among many different audiences and have loved every moment of it.

What Makes a Great Teacher

When you think of your educational background, more than likely you have had your fair share of awful, neutral and fabulous teachers. You may have had teachers who were just punching the clock to get their tenure, and you may have had teachers who were committed to their profession and embraced the investment it makes in future generations.

Perhaps you also know the right teacher can make all the difference. I know that has been true for me. For example, I chose physics as my first major in college because I had such an outstanding physics teacher in high school. (After one semester, it became clear that making an adjustment to that plan would be prudent. Studying physics was not a suitable path in life for me.)

But have you ever heard of the concept of a master teacher? A master teacher is one who not only knows their subject matter, but is also a master at communicating that content to students in ways that are engaging, memorable and even transformational.

That is who the Helper is to us. In that famous Last Supper teaching we have been studying, Jesus tells His followers, "These things I have spoken to you while abiding with you. But the Helper, the Holy Spirit, whom the Father will send in My name, He will teach you all things, and bring to your remembrance all that I said to you" (John 14:25–26).

Indeed, there has never existed a better teacher over the course of human history than the Helper. And I believe that what makes the Helper the Master Teacher is that He knows the intricacies and makeup of each student—meaning every single one of us. This is so important. In fact, it is what separates the true Master Teacher from the rest of us mere mortals who are practicing this essential craft.

During my experience teaching high school, I continually faced the question of how best to reach each student. Each one was so unique, and it was a fun challenge to figure out how to help each one acquire, digest and apply the material— even the boring stuff. Some days I did well, and some days I failed. I reached some students easily, and there were others with whom I never seemed to connect.

The Helper, our Master Teacher, does the teaching work masterfully. He knows how each of us learns. He understands our weak spots and what motivates us. He is dialed in to the lessons most essential to our identity and success in the class of life. Indeed, no one knows better than the Helper why we have been placed on the earth—what our purpose is and how we can best live out the synergy of our talents, assignments and purpose in concert with the seasons of our lives.

Teaching is about more than a transfer of information. In many respects, it is about transformation, and no one owns the territory of transformation better than the Helper. As it says in 2 Corinthians 3:18, "But we all, with unveiled face, beholding as in a mirror the glory of the Lord, are being transformed into the same image from glory to glory, just as from the Lord, the Spirit."

When Jesus tells His followers, then, that the Helper is a teacher who will remind them of all Jesus said, we can trust He puts a high premium on the whole teaching thing.

What the Helper Teaches

So, what do we learn from the Helper? To answer that question, let's first think about what we learned before bringing Jesus into our lives. At that point, we were learners of the world around us. We gathered information through our senses, through our interpretation of events, by noticing our shortcomings and successes and by paying attention to how experiences made us feel. All of this happened as we carried an elusive sense of purpose within us and witnessed varying degrees of pain, destruction, success and pleasure.

After bringing Jesus into our lives, however, the lessons we learned became altogether more vibrant, life-giving, divinely infused and distinctly truthful because of the nature of the Helper, our teacher.

Let's consider what the Helper teaches us.

How to Manage Life

I find the Helper is eager to teach me all kinds of practical things, such as:

- How to be a better wife
- How to write a book
- How to address insecurity
- How to learn from failure without getting obliterated by it
- How to lead in stressful situations
- How to embrace the right lessons and reject the wrong lessons
- How to be kind to unkind people
- How to travel with poise and flexibility
- How to unravel paradigms built on deception
- How to pay better attention

The Helper wants to have "deep in the weeds" access to my daily living to teach me practical things. This is an area where I need lots of help because I can be rather scatterbrained. One time, I even showed up to the airport a week early to fly to Dallas. After I tried to check in, the nice flight agent let me know I was a week early and that I should go home, relax and come back in a week. Being taught and given practical help by the Helper is a non-negotiable for me!

And speaking of being taught in the nitty-gritty, practical places of our lives, I do not think I have experienced anything more practical than being pregnant and delivering my children. Let's remember it was the Holy Spirit who

110

overshadowed Mary and helped her become pregnant with Jesus, the Son of God. I imagine the Helper taught Mary about being pregnant in lots of practical ways, especially given how difficult the pregnancy was for her for all kinds of cultural, historical and physical reasons. I can imagine Elizabeth, who was Mary's cousin and pregnant with John the Baptist at the time, was one way the Holy Spirit provided practical help to Mary in that season.

I want the Helper to be my teacher for lots of reasons, but if He can teach an unwed teenage mother to give birth in the difficult situation Mary faced, then it seems like good logic that He can teach us a host of things in our practical lives, too. The Helper brought what is divine into the daily reality of humans in the human form of Jesus. I, for one, admit I need as much divine help in my daily reality as I can get—and the more the better!

How to Translate Life Events

Because the Helper is the Spirit of truth, He enables us to learn the truth from situations—and when we do not have His help, we can be deceived. For example, I was invited to minister at a church a few years ago, and it was a pretty rough experience. The people were respectful, but I struggled to minister there. Everything was awkward—the communication was riddled with misunderstandings, the people were aloof and unresponsive, my speaking felt flat—and I returned home feeling discouraged and like I had failed.

A few weeks later, I learned the church was going through a severe financial strain. The pastor was in the middle of a family crisis, and the congregation was experiencing a localized mini-recession in their city.

Without the Helper's help, I had interpreted my experience at the church to be a personal rejection. However, if I had kept my eyes on the Helper, He may have helped me better understand what was happening around me. By trying to figure it out on my own, I became more vulnerable to deception and distortion.

How to Live Well

Let's consider again what I said earlier about the Helper knowing better than anyone how each of us is wired up. He knows our frame, our structure, our personality, our giftings, our weak spots and more. He knows how best to develop our potential and our talents, and He knows how to provide direction that is aligned with divine truth.

Given the quantity of self-help books on the market today, it is clear we have an innate longing to learn how to live, thrive and be fulfilled. Our world is overflowing with career advice, weight-loss tips, exercise suggestions, relationship counsel, get-ahead strategies, financial guidance and lots more. How should we now live? Who better to ask than the Helper, the One who made us and knows us better than we know ourselves?

What a Good Student Does

If the Helper is our teacher, then that means we are students of the Helper. This makes me want to be a really good student, and maybe it makes you want to be a good one, too.

But what does being a good student even mean?

Whenever I teach, I remind myself that a wide assortment of students could be sitting there, learning from me. Over the years, I have taught:

- Motivated students who had to work harder than most because their gifts were not "classroom friendly"
- Brilliant students whose curiosity challenged me to teach up, not down
- Smart students who, because of past experiences, thought they were stupid and sabotaged their own learning
- Students who were awesome at one subject—say, math—but struggled in another subject, like writing essays

Each student is unique and learns uniquely. Nevertheless, we are all students in the classroom of life, and with the Helper as our teacher, we want to learn how to be good students.

So, how do we do that? Here are a few pointers, taken from my years spent in education:

1. **Focus on the right subjects.** This is about sustaining high-grade truth and low-grade deception in our lives. Learning the wrong thing can result in poor application.

2. **Pay attention.** Take good notes and sit in the front row. Eliminate clutter and distractions. Prioritize your focus on the Helper.

3. **Bring your problems to the Helper.** It is okay to ask the teacher for help. You do not have to solve every problem on your own.

4. **Grow your trust.** When life throws a test at you, the Helper wants to help you pass it. Lean in and trust He is there and working to help you learn, grow and be effective.

5. **Respect the Helper.** Low respect leads to low learning.

6. **Keep at it.** You cannot learn everything in the first go-round, and the nature of learning means facing failures, hiccups and bumps along the way. Cultivate resilience.

7. **Check your perspective.** Learn to be transformed, not just informed. This is ultimately about becoming more like Jesus.

8. **Be curious.** Consider the awe and wonder of the world in which we live. Let the Helper use metaphors, like the daily sunrise as a reminder of God's faithful love to us, to help you learn and grow.

9. **Look deeper.** The Helper often works at levels not observable at a glance. Look below the surface. Be willing to dig deep.

10. **Be flexible.** Be willing to learn in different ways and not just how you normally like to learn. This is one of the marks of a lifelong learner. We all have our natural learning styles, but the Helper likes to use a variety of methods and conduits to reach and teach us.

What You Need to Remember

When it comes to learning, one of the most important ingredients is remembering stuff. (Just think of all those tests and quizzes you took in all those years of school!) But in our modern world, remembering things can get tricky, given the volume of information flying our way on any given day.

I forget heaps of things, and this used to stress me out. But I am managing my memory with a higher degree of priority these days. This means I may forget things that are not crazy important—like getting buttermilk at the grocery store—but stuff that is really important, like picking up an antibiotic for my son's strep throat, will get a higher level of attention. I also place a premium on Jesus' words to me so that I remember them and try to live them well. This is where the Helper steps up to the plate and helps me far beyond my natural abilities.

Jesus said the Helper would teach us all things, but He also said the Helper would remind us of all Jesus says to us. Check it out again: "The Helper . . . will teach you all things, and bring to your remembrance all that I said to you" (John 14:26).

Consider the timing here. Jesus and His eleven disciples were going to finish that special meal, the Last Supper, and then they were going to walk out the door to go to the Garden of Gethsemane. There, Jesus would be betrayed by Judas.

Now, if you are like me, when you go through a traumatic event, it is easy to forget everything else. For example, I was excited to meet up with one of my lifetime friends to do some snowboarding recently. We had worked out our family schedules and pulled together the monumental task of a joint ski trip. On the first afternoon, we met up for a few quick runs and then formulated our plans for the next day. I was totally pumped—but then I dislocated my shoulder. It happened on the first run of the day, and I was in such severe pain that I forgot everything else—all of our plans— and could focus only on getting my shoulder back into its socket as quickly as possible.

So when Jesus said the Helper would remind His followers of His words, consider how comforting that truth was in light of what they were about to face. His followers were about to go through some of the most intense and traumatic few days they would experience in their lives. And immediately before it happened, Jesus gave them one of the most concentrated, intimate training times He had ever given them. He gave them a massive amount of information—all of it important, none of which should be forgotten. Given the impending events—His arrest, trial and scourging; their abandonment of Him; His crucifixion, burial, resurrection and ascension; oh, and then Pentecost—it would have been easy for all of Jesus' teachings to slip their minds.

Yet Jesus told them the Helper would come to them and "bring to [their] remembrance" (John 14:26) all He had said to them. What a gift He offered them through that.

Here is what that means for us. When we go through stressful times, those are prime opportunities to invite the Helper closer—to let Him be involved in our lives and to ask Him to increase our sensitivity to His presence. In those difficult seasons, the Helper is there to remind us what Jesus says.

Now, the word Jesus used for *remind* here in the Greek is used less than ten times in the whole New Testament and only twice in the gospels—once when Peter remembered Jesus told him he would deny Him (see Luke 22:61) and then here in John 14:26.

I find all of this comforting, and I hope you do, too. As I write this, my life is overflowing with things I need to do, and the truth is that this never seems to change. If I am not careful, my life can turn into one giant to-do list, going from task to task, deadline to deadline and event to event. In all of the hustle and bustle, I can easily forget what God speaks to me in my morning Bible-and-prayer times. And yet I cannot count the number of times the Helper has reminded me in the midst of a busy day about something Jesus said during that morning time with Him.

I have also experienced the Helper nudging me to write out a verse or phrase from my morning prayer time on a card to carry with me through the day. Or to capture part of a verse on my phone and set it as my lock screen so whenever I check my phone for something during the day, the words are right there to encourage me. Sometimes the Helper reminds me of something I heard in a sermon or spiritual conversation or brings to mind a Bible verse that speaks to a situation in my day.

All of these experiences support what Jesus said about the Helper—that He will remind us of Jesus' words. There is such constant support and help available to us!

What Matters Most

As we finish out this chapter, let me offer one last observation from this passage. When Jesus says, "The Helper, the

Holy Spirit, whom the Father will send in my name . . ." (John 14:26), it is the first time in John's gospel that Jesus refers to the Helper by His formal name, the Holy Spirit. In fact, Jesus only calls the Holy Spirit by that formal name one other time in John's gospel, and it is at the end of the book, when He breathes on the disciples after the resurrection and says, "Receive the Holy Spirit" (John 20:22).

Before this mention of the Holy Spirit's formal name in the Last Supper teaching, Jesus used two other terms to introduce the Holy Spirit, both of which we have already explored: Helper and Spirit of truth. He had also, by that point, taught several things that this Helper and Spirit of truth will do for us, such as teach us, remind us, help us and even parent us. Only after having introduced these other names and activities does Jesus share the more formal name of the Holy Spirit with His disciples.

Perhaps we are to glean from this that we are meant to get comfortable with the Helper's presence and activity in our daily lives before turning to concerns about formal titles and theology. Just something to think about.

Inspect, Reflect, Apply

1. Who was your favorite teacher in school, and why?

2. From what teacher did you learn the most, and why?

3. What lessons do you find easiest to learn from the Helper?

4. What lessons are more difficult for you to learn from the Helper?

5. How might your past educational experiences impact the way you learn from the Helper today?

6. Educators believe people learn best through listening, watching or doing. How does the Helper invite you to learn in these ways?

7. How does the Helper remind you of the things Jesus says?

Time to Learn

"Ruth, if you could learn anything in the world without getting hurt or failing, what would it be?"

Naomi always asked these piercing questions I could never quite answer with glib detachment. She seemed to plumb the depths of my thoughts and personality, helping me learn new things about myself.

"Well, I certainly have a bucket list of things I'd like to *accomplish* while I'm alive," I said. "But what would I most enjoy learning? That's a really interesting question. What about you?"

I was deflecting the question, and she knew it. But she played along.

"If I could learn anything without getting hurt or failing," she said, "I'd learn to how to use a potter's wheel to make beautiful pottery."

I looked at Naomi's hands. They were gentle, nimble, strong and worn. She didn't fret about her nail polish getting chipped, and I knew from her beautiful garden that it didn't bother her in the least to get her hands dirty. But this pottery interest caught me by surprise.

"I don't really see you as a pottery type of person," I said. "You seem more interested in flowers, birds and coffee than getting messy, with clay flying everywhere from a spinning potter's wheel."

"Ruth, although we are becoming good friends, you'll find I'm full of interesting surprises. Now, back to my original question. What would you choose to learn if you couldn't fail or get hurt? No more deflecting!"

I paused, thinking about it. Then I said, "I'd like to learn how to fly with a wingsuit."

"A wing what?"

"A wingsuit! I saw a YouTube video once where this guy jumped off a cliff, and instead of dropping like a rock, he was gliding through the air in this wing-and-web suit thing. It was totally cool. I would love to learn how to do that."

I could tell by the look on Naomi's face that she was far from amused, but I reminded her that after meeting her in the grocery store, our first adventure was bungee jumping. A wingsuit was just a different way of traveling in the air.

"Well, as your friend who is enjoying the adventure of getting to know you," she said, "I appreciate that you would find wingsuits and cliff-gliding to be worth learning. As for me, bungee jumping was pretty extreme, and I prefer to keep my hands in the dirt. But if you would consider taking some pottery lessons with me, I'll watch a few YouTube videos on wingsuits with you."

Because of this conversation, we began to learn new things. I agreed to sign up for six weeks of pottery classes with her. And while I could tell Naomi was pleased I'd agreed to join her in that adventure, I knew she wasn't as eager to share my enthusiasm for wingsuits and gliding. Nevertheless, our agreement held fast, and once I found some local classes that taught the ins and outs of using a wingsuit and jumping protocols and included a few amateur jumps, she agreed to join me.

Pottery class starts 7:30 p.m. Thurs, Smith Community College. Don't be late—meet you there.

Naomi's text message called out my weak spot for being late, so I replied, *Okeydokey, Thurs, 7:42 p.m. at SCC :).*

When I showed up, all of the new students huddled along the sides of the room, waiting for the instructor to start teaching. Naomi caught my eye, and we chuckled at the fun we were about to have from these learning adventures. Truth be known, I love to learn, so the opportunity to explore some new things with her was high-grade awesome in my book.

Zing!

A little while later, my clay lump flew off the potter's wheel at warp speed and stuck on the wall, leaving a cool 3-D design that I pretended to have planned. Naomi chuckled under her breath because she knew I hadn't listened well—I'd gotten distracted by all the random books in the room. In contrast, Naomi listened with laser-sharp focus to everything the instructor said and followed each step with precision.

"Ruth, if you ask me for help, I'm more than happy to help you," she said, reminding me of our conversation a while back about my struggle to do that very thing—ask for help.

Naomi was never condescending, but she paid attention really well. Helping was also one of her core strengths, along with teaching, so when she made that offer to help me this time, I readily accepted it.

"First of all, roll up your sleeves, tie your hair and put your rings in your pocket," she said. "Then wedge your clay."

She gave me step-by-step instructions, and I appreciated her ability to translate the technical information the instructor gave into practical steps I could apply. This is something else I love about Naomi: She can take something a person has made complicated and turn it into something simple to apply. I am learning to pay attention to her because I've learned she is an exceptional teacher.

Our first night of pottery class was fun, gritty, muddy and informative. I could tell the next few weeks were going to be a great learning adventure. Not only would I get to learn about shaping clay into something beautiful, but I'd also get to know Naomi more.

Over the course of six weeks, Naomi mastered the potter's wheel with deft agility and became the instructor's assistant in the class. He even offered to pay her to join his next class to help floundering students! I think he saw how much she helped me, a fumbling and halfway-interested learner, and was impressed with her ability to work not only with dirt clay but also human clay. I was proud Naomi was my friend.

Even so, she declined his offer.

"You are kind to give me the opportunity to assist you," she said. "Thank you for the compliment. But I must decline in order to keep my agreement with Ruth for our wingsuit lessons."

The instructor looked at her quizzically when he heard the word *wingsuit*.

I was standing nearby, so I chimed in. "Naomi and I made a bargain that I would take pottery lessons with her and she would take wingsuit-gliding lessons with me."

"What are wingsuit-gliding lessons?" he asked.

"They're so cool!" I said. "You put on a special suit, with webbing from the sleeves to the legs and between the legs.

Then you jump off a cliff, spread out your arms and legs and glide through the air, safely landing on your feet."

The wingsuit thing didn't appear to be his cup of tea, as upon hearing my explanation, he bustled off to his car.

The following week, I picked up Naomi for our first wingsuit-gliding lesson. The group was packed with adventure junkies like me. Clearly, it wasn't the place for the more cautious and risk-averse types—except Naomi, of course, my loyal friend who was committed to uphold her part of our agreement.

When I caught her eye at the start of the class, I caught a glimpse of that knowing smirk she gave me before her first bungee jump. I knew we were going to have some premium-quality fun.

One of the downsides of having instructors for thrill-seeking subjects is they often lack real teaching skills. They're in it for the adventure—because they love experiencing the thrill of the actual event—not because they love to teach.

Naomi, in contrast, can teach anything.

That first day, I expected to first learn a bit about the wing-suit and how to approach a jump, but the instructor just said, "When you jump into your suit, just zip it and rip it. It'll be a blast—see you at the cliff!"

On that note, he and the rest of the adventure junkies sauntered out of the classroom, tossing out the names of local bars where they were going to meet up afterward.

And that was the end of our first class. It lasted a whole thirty seconds.

Thankfully, there was an administrative person in the classroom, distributing and collecting insurance and legal waivers, so Naomi asked, "Do you have any information on the suits or amateur cliff locations where we'll be jumping?"

Again, I was proud to have her as my friend. She always found a way to put ground under my feet, rather than letting me float off on some wingsuit feat that carried a high potential for being totally disastrous.

"Thank you for asking responsible questions," the assistant said. "Here's a handout for all of the local stores that supply wingsuits. Our next class will be at the Smith Community College mini-cliff, behind the campus administrative building, at ten a.m. on Saturday. Please sign and date all the waivers, supplying your health insurance details as well. We need all of these papers signed and properly filled out for the amateur jump on Saturday."

From there, Naomi and I checked out the local wingsuit suppliers, learned a boatload about wingsuits and showed up on Saturday with our paperwork filled out and signed. About half the class showed up, and the instructor was more than thirty minutes late, which inspired no degree of confidence in Naomi.

"Let's suit up!" the instructor said when he arrived—and that was the sum total of our second lesson.

"I wonder how a person gets certified to be a wingsuit instructor?" Naomi muttered.

I was beginning to share her disappointment with our experience so far, but I still maintained my enthusiasm for this new adventure that was certain to be thrilling with a hearty dose of dangerous.

The other people in the class fumbled to get into their suits, but as I watched Naomi, I could tell she'd done her homework. With nimble grace, she slipped into her wingsuit and then said, "Ruth, I watched a few wingsuit lessons and learned some helpful pointers. First of all, there's some vocabulary about your wingsuit that will be helpful to know. . . ."

Naomi was prepared for our adventure and eager to help me succeed. She gave me all of the instructions I needed and inspected my wingsuit to ensure it was properly fitted and flawless. The rest of our class was only semi-interested in learning what she knew, and the majority of them didn't even show up with a suit. The instructor, meanwhile, had gotten distracted by a cute blonde who had forgotten her wingsuit.

In the end, Naomi and I were the only ones who did the first amateur leap. For me, it was a totally religious experience.

I watched Naomi jump first—after she went through a wingsuit checklist she'd made for inspection and execution, of course, which she then handed to me to complete, as well. After she jumped, I followed, then caught a gentle breeze that carried me. At first, I was crazy nervous, but as I watched Naomi flow with the wind ahead of me, I began to emulate her and found myself synced with the wind in a beautiful synergy. Like I said, it was a spiritual experience, serene and placid and like nothing I'd ever known before.

When I finally landed safely, I asked Naomi what she thought of her first wingsuit jump.

She simply said, "Divine."

7

Can I Get a Witness?

What does love look like? It has the hands to help others. It has the feet to hasten to the poor and needy. It has eyes to see misery and want. It has the ears to hear the sighs and sorrows of men. That is what love looks like.

SAINT AUGUSTINE

"When the Helper comes, whom I will send to you from the Father, that is the Spirit of truth who proceeds from the Father, He will testify about Me, and you will testify also, because you have been with Me from the beginning."

JOHN 15:26–27

Have you ever had to testify at a trial? My first exposure to courts, legal proceedings, witnesses and the like were the black-and-white *Perry Mason* episodes that a local TV channel ran back in the day. Perry Mason was an attorney on an old series about criminal justice—and to be honest, the series always creeped me out. The action was slow, the music was eerie and the dialogue was tedious. I can still remember the music and the way Perry looked when he questioned a witness on the stand.

I never liked the way the program made me feel queasy and unsettled. So it should come as no surprise that I had an initial resistance to the words Jesus says to His followers in that Last Supper conversation that circled around the subject of testifying. He says, "When the Helper comes, whom I will send to you from the Father, that is the Spirit of truth who proceeds from the Father, He will testify about Me, and you will testify also, because you have been with Me from the beginning" (John 15:26–27).

What's This Testifying Business?

Jesus says the Helper will testify, or bear witness, about Jesus. In our language, He is saying the Helper will communicate to us who Jesus is.

In some respects, this is like what happens when I describe one of my friends to you. Let's try it. I have a friend—we will call her Suzanne to keep it anonymous—and she is entirely amazing. She is brilliant, caring, honest, loyal, strong and confident. She has survived all kinds of hardships and difficulties, stemming from her childhood through her teen years and well into middle age. I would venture to say there is virtually nothing Suzanne cannot do—she is amazing, and I am honored to be her friend.

Now, I just described to you a good friend I have known for more than ten years. I gave you a witness, or description, of who she is based on my experience of her and my conversations with her. This is a simple way to understand the words *witness* or *testify*. When we think about the Helper bearing witness, or testifying, to us about Jesus, let's consider that this means He is going to describe Jesus to us based on His knowledge of Jesus.

The word *testify*, also translated "bear witness," comes from the Greek word *martureo*, where we get our English word *martyr*. Now, before we jump to the conclusion that this passage is inviting us to die for our faith, we have to understand that when Jesus used this word with His disciples, the massive persecution against His followers had not yet broken out. At the time, no Christians were being boiled in oil, lit on fire in Rome or eaten by lions in the Colosseum of Rome for public entertainment. The idea of a martyr being a person who died for their faith came *after* these words Jesus offered in John 15. When Jesus spoke of the Helper being someone who would testify— *martureo*—He simply meant the Helper would describe Jesus to us.

Testifying, or witnessing, also carries the notion of demonstration here. For example, a person who is a witness in a trial may be asked to demonstrate what they saw related to a car accident, perhaps giving an account of what happened using models. When I grocery shop, many times I find a demonstration being given of a product someone wants me to buy—a blender, a vacuum, a sample. Related to this passage, then, the Helper demonstrates who Jesus is by helping us experience the reality of Jesus in our daily living.

For example, I recently went for a jog outside after almost a year of not jogging. While this could have been an excruciating experience, instead it was amazing. As I jogged, it began to rain and became kind of misty. Then I felt the Holy Spirit begin to talk with me about some personal stuff with which I had been struggling, helping me see things more clearly and from a more healthy perspective. The care the Helper demonstrated toward me during that jog was an expression of Jesus' love.

What's more, the Helper empowers us to demonstrate Jesus as well. Two passages indicate this:

> "And you will testify also, because you have been with Me from the beginning."
>
> John 15:27

> "But you will receive power when the Holy Spirit has come upon you; and you shall be My witnesses both in Jerusalem, and in all Judea and Samaria, and even to the remotest part of the earth."
>
> Acts 1:8

This is sometimes where we get into hot water with accusations about our being hypocrites. Throughout history, there are more than enough examples of people who professed to follow Jesus but fell short when it came to demonstrating Jesus' teachings or values. It is one thing to talk the walk, but it is an entirely different level of intimacy when we give the Helper permission to help us walk the talk. I find it helps to remember these words often attributed to Saint Francis: "Preach the Gospel at all times, and when necessary, use words." Let's be sure our behaviors and values are in sync with our words.

What Would You Have Done?

Recently, I had an opportunity to do just that—to let my walk mirror my talk—on my way home from the grocery store. I was about to turn toward my neighborhood on a bright and sunny day around noon when I saw a lady walking with a limp. When I went to round the corner, she waited for me to pass. I noticed her face screwed up in a kind of grimace. She looked cranky!

I kept driving toward my house, thinking how cranky she looked, when I remembered her limp. Perhaps she looked cranky because she was in pain. Immediately, I had a quick flash of insight: *Go pray for her.* Then my brain and the Helper entered into a brief but intense conflict that went something like this:

Helper: Go pray for her.

Me: Are you kidding? I have no clue who she is.

Helper: Who cares? Go pray for her.

Me: She's going to think I'm weird.

Helper: You *are* weird. Go pray for her.

Me: I know You want me to do this spontaneous prayer thing for people more often. I'll do it next time.

Helper: Stop putting Me off.

131

Me: Later—I promise.

Helper: You keep telling Me that, but when is later? Do it!

By this time, I was in my neighborhood, so I did a 180 with my car. I drove back and parked on the side of the road.

Once I had turned my car around, I was fully committed to catching up with the lady and offering to pray for her. After I parked, I hopped out of the car and jogged up the sidewalk, looking for her. Sure enough, I saw her through the trees in the distance, walking with her back toward me.

I thought to myself, *Don't run up to her, because you'll probably spook her. When you get closer, slow down and try to catch your breath.*

When I slowed down upon approaching her, she turned around and started walking toward me. I was feeling nervous, but I felt this voice in my heart say, *Don't jump ahead of Me. Slow down and pay attention—maybe even get some help—before you just dive in.* That sounded like good advice, so I slowed my thoughts and walking pace.

Putting on a smile, I walked up to the lady and said, "Hi! My name is Sarah, and I live just around the corner. I was on my way home and noticed you taking a walk with a bit of a limp. Are you feeling okay?"

"Sure. It's nice to meet you, Sarah," she said. "I'm Pat, and I'm feeling fine. Thanks for asking."

"Pat, it seemed you were limping a bit on your walk. Are you in any pain?"

"No, I'm fine."

"Any problems with your joints?"

"Well, I have a small amount of arthritis, but not anything major."

"Is your digestion good? How's your heart? Lungs healthy?"

"Yes, my digestion is fine and my heart is strong. No breathing problems either."

"That's wonderful!" I said. "How's your family? Kids doing well?"

As I asked my twenty questions, I also tried to listen to the Helper guiding me and directing my questions so I could connect with Pat.

"My kids are good," she said. "Do you have kids?"

"Yes, I have three kids who go to the middle school just up the street in our neighborhood. Hey, Pat, would you mind if I prayed for the arthritis stuff?"

"Well, yes, you can pray, and thanks for offering," she said. "But go ahead and pray on your own, because I have my own type of faith. I appreciate your concern."

By this point, we had come to the corner and I could tell she was finished with our friendly conversation.

"Okeydokey, Pat," I said. "I'll pray for the arthritis stuff, and thanks so much for the nice chat and your time."

When I got in my car, I heard in my heart, *Great job being obedient!* I did not feel like a failure for not getting to pray with Pat on the spot. Even though there was not an outright demonstration in the moment of God's presence, power or healing, I had been willing to put myself in a position where the Helper *could* demonstrate or be a witness through me of who Jesus is.

On the flip side, I can appreciate how scary it is to put yourself out there like I did with Pat. It can be so scary that it becomes easy to dismiss that internal voice or prompting to go ahead and bear witness in a conversation, no matter if it is with a stranger, an acquaintance, a friend or a relative.

Let's be mindful, too, that all action with no words can be a hopeless expression of empty transformation. For example, Paul says, "How then will they call on Him in whom they have not believed? How will they believe in Him whom they have not heard? And how will they hear without a preacher?" (Romans 10:14). While I am a huge advocate of making our love for Jesus practical through charitable behaviors and financial contributions, let's never downgrade the importance of using words to share the reality of who Jesus is and the immensity of Jesus' personal love for us with the people around us. All actions with no words becomes a slippery slope for deception, and all words with no action signals the puffy smoke of hypocrisy that can choke out any possibility for someone to connect in an authentic way with Jesus.

I want to be a conduit for people to connect with Jesus in meaningful and transformational ways, and I want others to want this, too. (I hope it is what you want!) However, I do not see how this happens without divine help—in other words, without the help of the Holy Spirit. So, how do we cooperate with the Helper's help? Is it even possible to connect people to Jesus without turning into a mutant religious zealot? What might this look like in our daily living?

What If You Start with Coffee?

Let's start with this question: Do you have something you love and talk about with others? In my life, I savor and enjoy coffee. I relish sitting with a friend to share a rich and deep conversation over a tasty cup of joe. I was on a trip to

Ethiopia several years ago and made one of my deepest spiritual friendships over many macchiatos. In fact, a lot of this book finds its roots in those conversations, and to this day I love connecting with my friend about the Holy Spirit over macchiatos. Those discussions are nothing less than electric!

Not only do I like to have these rich conversations over coffee, but I am also a coffee aficionado. My husband even calls me an addict and a coffee snob. (He may be right on the snob part.)

Here is what I have noticed: I am also a coffee evangelist. One of the coolest things I love to do is to make friends with a barista and then bring in my favorite coffee to share with them. It is a coffee blend roasted by my good buddy Andy. I bring my portable coffeemaker with me into the coffee shop and brew a quick cup for the barista—a role reversal, to be sure.

When I am making up the quick brew, I also tell the barista what kind of coffee I am using. I become an evangelist for my favorite roasting and coffee supply outlet in the whole world. The coffee is nothing less than heavenly. And when the barista starts to say how delicious it tastes, I tell them how they can get a steady supply of the awesome elixir from Andy, roaster extraordinaire.

If you think about it, we are all evangelists for products, stores, experiences and more. It does not just apply to coffee. We advertise what we believe in all the time, whether it be a certain brand of shoes, a band we love, the car we drive, the sports jerseys we wear or the causes we advertise on our disposable water bottles.

When we get into this same groove with the Helper, we "advertise" Jesus—but not for branding purposes. Rather, we are telling people who Jesus is and what Jesus does.

What could this look like in our daily living?

Let's think about this within the framework of having a spiritual conversation. We can get so jittery when it comes to talking about Jesus with someone who is not a follower of Him—particularly if we are introverts. Our culture says we are supposed to be tolerant and that any overt or heavy-duty proselytizing is nothing less than offensive, rude or repulsive. Talking about Jesus can get dicey.

It gets even more difficult to share the reality of Jesus with someone when we are not attentive to who that person is or what their needs might be. When we start treating people as objects or projects rather than human beings, things can go rogue super fast.

By way of example, I was in Israel one time and our tour guide was really smart. He knew all the historical artifacts and Bible references. He was totally on his game—even brilliant.

A few ladies in our group were witnessing to him and telling him about Jesus.

"Are you a Jew?" they asked.

"Yes, I was born Jewish," he said.

"Then do you know about Jesus?"

"Yes, I'm aware you believe Jesus is the Messiah," he said.

In the back of the bus, I heard one of them say, "I'm going to win this guy for Christ!"

At the end of our trip, he prayed with them to receive Jesus and they returned to the bus excited. However, I saw the tour guide, once the ladies were away from the bus, wink at the bus driver. And in that one wink, I figured it all out. This guy had been down the "salvation prayer" road before. There had no doubt been a host of other well-intentioned

Christians who had witnessed to this tour guide before. He knew how it went: If you get "saved," your tips go up.

While I appreciate those ladies and their good intentions, their execution was misguided. They saw the tour guide as a checkbox or notch on their belt rather than as a human with needs, desires, hopes, hurts, ambitions and shortcomings.

Rather than frame the idea of witnessing, sharing, advertising or testifying about Jesus in the context of proselytizing or creating converts, let's think about it with an organic mindset, as a backdrop to our daily interactions. Again, let's think about it in the terms of having spiritual conversations.

A spiritual conversation is simply a chat about something spiritual in the course of our daily living, even with people who do not necessarily believe the same way we do. Some things that can be helpful to do when having spiritual conversations are:

- **Listen.** Ask questions. Pay attention. Demonstrate sincere interest in the other person, not merely seeing them as a potential convert but as someone deeply loved by the Helper.
- **Show respect.** Attitudes that betray an agenda of winning, convincing, coercing or shaming do not belong in these conversations.
- **Avoid pressured words.** *Should* and *ought to* are unhelpful words in this context.
- **Be present.** Sometimes it does not help to have all the answers. Oftentimes, a person just needs you to be present and loving toward them.

- **Include followers.** Share with someone else who follows Jesus what the Helper has been teaching you.
- **Be sensitive.** Sometimes people are not in a place where this kind of conversation helps. A recent death in the family, for instance, could signal a time to be extra sensitive and supportive.

What If You Just Connect?

Another way to give the Holy Spirit permission to testify through you is to express something God has done in your life that might match a need in the other person's life. For instance, sometimes on airplanes I am seated next to people who share challenges they are facing. One time a person was telling me about their employer, and I remembered a situation I once faced when a supervisor asked me to do something that was not comfortable for me. My husband and I prayed about it, and after several days, I learned my supervisor had changed his mind. I shared this experience with my seatmate on the plane and asked if I could pray with him about his work challenge. He said it was fine for me to pray, so I went ahead, right there on the plane. I could sense the Helper's presence as we prayed, and my seatmate became less anxious and more peaceful.

Let's never minimize these kinds of opportunities, thinking we are only a witness if someone prays the sinner's prayer with us to receive salvation. Consider what Paul says in 1 Corinthians 3:7: "So then neither the one who plants nor the one who waters is anything, but God who causes the growth." Sometimes we get to plant a seed about Jesus in someone's heart; sometimes we get to water a seed that has already been planted; and sometimes we get to pray with a person to receive Jesus into their lives. No matter what our role is with a person, God is the One who causes a person to grow closer to Jesus.

Consider, too, what Jesus says in Mark 4:28: "The soil produces crops by itself; first the blade, then the head, then the mature grain in the head." Here, Jesus teaches us that plants are not the only things that take time to create crops, first through the blade, then the head and then the mature grain. People grow incrementally in their relationship with Jesus, too.

Let me share one final story about sharing Jesus in an unlikely situation. When I was in my late teens, in the late 1980s, my parents took me to China for our first exploratory trip to the Orient. At that time, China was recovering from the atrocities of its cultural revolution, and the country was nowhere near as developed as it is today.

We were in some remote city on a boat cruise that was far from pleasurable. It was sticky, humid and hot. What is more, the people did not wear deodorant. Everyone reeked of garlic, such that it was almost impossible to share any lengthy or undistracted conversation. They were serving hot tea, did not have any ice, and there were mosquitos everywhere.

I can imagine it is not hard for you to believe this nineteen-year-old bratty American diva was more than cranky when a nice Chinese lady came over and started speaking Mandarin.

I looked at her and thought, *Do I look like I speak Mandarin —seriously?* Nevertheless, I was taught to be polite and mind my manners, so I found a translator to help us communicate.

The woman was eager to hear why we were in China, and when I started talking with her about Jesus, she was clueless. Her ignorance was astounding to me, but I forged ahead. By the end of our conversation, she prayed with me to receive Jesus into her life. We were able to give her a Mandarin Bible and a plan for reading the Bible every day.

My point in sharing this story is to demonstrate that the Helper asks only to have access to our world and the people with whom we interact. Let's be better at yielding than hesitating—or even opposing—the Helper as a witness in our daily living. There are lots of ways the Helper can give testimony and bear witness to who Jesus is and what Jesus does through us.

As a closing thought, I will share with you that I have had conversations with strangers who asked me difficult questions about Jesus, about why bad things happened in their lives, about the reliability of the Bible benchmarked against historical documents. They are too numerous to describe. But with all of them, I never pretend to have all of the answers. It is not uncommon for me to admit I do not know everything, nor do I pretend to think I do.

What I have found most important in these spiritual conversations is to be genuinely loving, sincerely authentic and compassionately caring toward the people with whom I am talking. Their lives are every bit as important to the Helper as my life is. With the Helper working through us to connect people to Jesus, let's be agents of genuine love.

Inspect, Reflect, Apply

1. How did you come to know and experience Jesus? What were some important components for you to connect with Him?

2. In what ways has the Helper connected you with Jesus at different times in your life?

3. What are some testimonies you can give from your life of God's power, presence or love?

4. Have you ever struggled to share Jesus with someone? What did you do when that happened?

5. Have you ever found yourself treating people like objects or projects when sharing with them about Jesus? How has that turned out?

6. Ask the Helper to open your eyes to see opportunities to share with others what Jesus has done in your life.

Witness

"Ruth, let's do a cruise," Naomi said, dropping a bomb into our conversation. "It would be so much fun! We could meet new people, see cool stuff and do some fun excursions together."

"Are you serious?" I said. "No way! I can't think of anything worse than being stuck on a boat, surrounded by strangers and endless superficial conversations. I enjoy our friendship, to be sure, but a cruise sounds like a personalized hell. Thanks, but no thanks."

"I think this could be a total *blast*," Naomi persisted, "so I'm going to talk with your husband and see if he'll give you a Christmas and birthday present for a cruise—something short and fun!"

"If he agrees, I'll drop my teeth," I said.

Clearly, we were having a role reversal in this conversation. Normally, I'm the impulsive and adventurous one. Naomi's idea for this cruise caught me off guard.

Nevertheless, she forged ahead and talked with my husband, and soon I found myself on a six-day cruise through the Norwegian fjords. At least the location and geography were interesting. But the boat was exactly as I had expected: crawling with people. While Naomi was in heaven, I looked for any nook, cranny or crevice I could find that was cozy, quiet and isolated. But it was impossible to find such a place. People were everywhere, and I had no escape—unless I jumped overboard.

"Now, Ruth, I know that you're a person who needs her personal space," explained Naomi over breakfast on the first day at sea on the *Selskap*, which was Norwegian for *party*, "so I'll go ahead and give you the list of today's activities. Of course, you're welcome to join me in any of my selections. I've signed up for a yoga class, along with the Adventures in Appetizers class with the ship's chef. This afternoon, there's an excursion on a Zodiac to explore the more remote fjords. Tonight, our formal dinner reservation is at table 237 for the 7:30 seating. Isn't this exciting?"

Naomi was brimming with energy, and I was happy for her, but I was also trying to figure out how to navigate this floating hell. Suffice it to say, Naomi did her first day's schedule alone while I looked on the boat for a serene and reclusive place to spend the day.

When we met up for dinner that night, I learned table 237 had six other diners. I was forced to choose between being surly and rude or engaging and superficial. Of course, Naomi jumped in with both feet, introducing herself and meeting each person who would be dining with us for the next few evenings.

I decided to try putting my best foot forward and turned to the young woman on my right.

"My name is Ruth," I said, "and I'm from the United States. Where are you from?"

"Nice to meet you," she said. "My name is Antje. This is my friend Stefan, and we are on a special student excursion from our university in Leipzig, Germany. Our degree plan pays for us to visit neighboring countries with a cultural exchange program. But I'm eager to talk with you, as I've never had opportunity to speak with an American before."

"How did you learn English so well?" I asked.

"Part of our high school education is to learn a second language, and I chose English. Thank you for the compliment! Do you mind if I ask you a few questions, since this is my first chance to speak face-to-face with an American?"

"Sure—fire away!" I said, relieved I wouldn't have to carry the burden of sustaining a shallow conversation.

"What does it mean, *fire away*?" she asked.

"Sorry. That's American slang for *go ahead*. What would you like to talk about?"

"Well, can you please tell me where you're from, and maybe a little bit about your family and education?"

No superficial talk about the weather—yippee!

"I was born in a town in the western part of the United States, and I'm the third of four children," I said. "My father was a university professor of geology, and my mother was a schoolteacher. Education was an important value in our family. All of my brothers and sisters have at least a master's degree. And my mother recently died."

Upon the mention of my mom, I could feel myself getting choked up, and I started to panic. That's the problem with grief—it hits you like a sledgehammer when you least expect it.

"I was with Ruth when her mom passed," Naomi said, coming to my rescue before I had to excuse myself to the restroom for an emotional meltdown.

"Where is Leipzig?" she asked, deftly changing the subject.

"It's in former East Germany," Antje said, "and because of the Communist system that existed there for several decades, the economy is severely depressed. Our excursion on this cruise is financed by the government to invest in the upcoming generation for better economic and cultural integration into Western Europe."

I was intrigued to hear she grew up in East Germany. What could that have been like for her?

"Do you consider yourselves to be religious?" Antje asked. "I'm asking because in my country, we were trained to be atheists. In contrast, I hear that Americans can be hyper-religious. Please don't take offense at my question."

"What a fascinating question," Naomi replied. "It depends on who you ask from America, though. But since you're asking us, let me take a minute to describe an important ingredient in my worldview.

"Ruth and I would be considered strong believers in Jesus. I'm a believer not merely because of an intellectual dogma that I find convincing, but because of a deep connection and relationship that I experience with Jesus."

Antje was quiet for a minute, digesting Naomi's words.

Then Stefan, Antje's friend, chimed in. "What do you mean when you talk about a deep connection and relationship with Jesus? I've studied the Christian religion before, but I haven't heard this religion spoken about with these kinds of words before."

"Well, there's certainly a wide range of what Christianity can mean to various people," Naomi said. "But I believe the simple yet powerful core of Christianity revolves around the central truth that God deeply loves humanity, not because humans are so lovable but for the central truth that God is love. And He sent Jesus into humanity as the full expression of His love in human form. Clearly, Jesus' death was the supreme expression of genuine love. Of ultimate importance is the fact that Jesus was raised from the dead. Jesus' life, death and resurrection afford each person the opportunity to connect with God in a deeply intimate and personal relationship—a spiritual connection that is grounded in God's love for us."

The air around us sparked with electricity as Naomi spoke, and when I looked at Antje and Stefan, I could see they were not only absorbing what she had just explained, but they were also mesmerized and captivated. It wasn't just her words. The atmosphere felt charged with love.

There was a long pause, and I knew it was a sacred and holy moment. I didn't want to distract Antje or Stefan from processing Naomi's words and presence, so I stayed silent.

Then our waiter chimed in.

"What would you like for your appetizer?" he asked.

We were all snapped back to the present reality that we were seated together at table 237 on the *Selskap* ship, preparing to eat our first dinner together.

Each of us gave the waiter our selection, and after the waiter had finished collecting everyone's order, Stefan resumed the conversation.

"I'm curious about the words that you've shared with us, Naomi, and I'd like to ask you some more questions, perhaps after dinner. We could all watch the sunset over the beautiful fjords on one of the upper decks."

"I'd like nothing more than that, Stefan," Naomi said. "Thank you so much for your interest—I really look forward to our conversation."

I love that nothing catches Naomi off guard and that she's totally authentic. Because she's so comfortable with herself, she makes everyone around her feel comfortable and accepted, too—even a person who just met her. She makes them feel like they've known her a long time and that she's trustworthy, safe and wise.

After dinner, we met up with Stefan and Antje on the *Moro* deck, and Antje said, "Naomi, your words at dinner were like nothing I've ever heard or experienced in my life. Would you please help me to experience what you were talking about at dinner?"

"Me, too," chimed Stefan.

"What I love so much about Jesus," explained Naomi, "is that He eagerly welcomes each of us to not only learn about Him from an intellectual perspective, but also to spiritually connect with Him. Stefan and Antje, I believe this is what your hearts are longing for, but you've had a difficult time trying to express this desire."

"Naomi, I'm not sure how," Stefan said, "but it's like you've known us all our lives and can read into the deepest parts of our hearts. Thank you for being so insightful and helpful. Yes, you're right. My heart has been searching, and I'd almost given up hope trying to find the answer to my longing."

Stefan's honesty and willingness to talk on such deep and spiritual levels made me appreciate my friendship with Naomi like never before. I knew she was wise, but her ability to point to Jesus as the answer to the longing in each person's heart was nothing short of miraculous. I watched the supernatural unfold before my eyes.

"Antje, how do you feel about our conversation up to this point?" Naomi asked.

"I am in complete agreement with Stefan, and I'd like to know what we can do next to experience what you've shared with us. Thank you for helping us so much!"

"Antje and Stefan, let's take a quiet moment to talk with Jesus," Naomi said. "I'd encourage you to take some time to think about any areas in your life that make it difficult for you to believe in Jesus and then surrender each of these areas. Sometimes people struggle to connect with Jesus because of some of their past behaviors and choices. At other times, people have struggled to connect with Jesus because they come to Him with an 'earner' mindset, thinking they have to deserve to have Jesus in their lives. Take a few minutes and consider what the obstacles might be for you, Stefan, and for you, Antje, and then surrender those obstacles and welcome Jesus into your life to be your best friend, premier guide and authority."

Antje and Stefan went to the rail of the ship and spent time in prayerful reflection, as Naomi had suggested. In the meantime, I sat on a deck chair and prayed for my new friends and the beginning of their relationship with Jesus.

During the rest of our cruise, Naomi and I enjoyed meeting up with Stefan and Antje on shore excursions and during dinner. Our conversations were rich, spiritual and nurturing. By the time the cruise came to an end, Antje and Stefan were locked into a deeply satisfying and spiritual relationship with Jesus, thanks to the divine guidance of Naomi, my friend. She bore an incredible witness to the life-giving relationship we can have with Jesus, and what seemed like a superficial six-day cruise turned into a transformative journey for all of us.

8

The Upgrade Advantage

Trying to do the Lord's work in your own strength is the most confusing, exhausting, and tedious of all work. But when you are filled with the Holy Spirit, then the ministry of Jesus just flows out of you.

CORRIE TEN BOOM

"But I tell you the truth, it is to your advantage that I go away; for if I do not go away, the Helper will not come to you; but if I go, I will send Him to you."

JOHN 16:7

When I was growing up, I loved to play sports—football at recess, softball in middle school and, of course, basketball.

To this day, I regret not playing volleyball in middle and high school. I tried out for cross country as a sophomore and learned that was not my cup of tea. Nevertheless, my experience in sports was well-rounded—especially compared to kids in today's world.

I am learning as my kids grow that the majority of sports-minded families concentrate on one sport so their children can advance in that one area. I have heard of boys who were started in a sport—hockey, football, soccer—as young as three years old so that by the time they turned ten, they had honed their single-sport skills with such proficiency that they carried a major advantage over their peers who had diversified their participation in sports.

That is not the only area where we are looking for an advantage in modern life. Almost all airlines now have special groups that provide ways to upgrade tickets. We hear of people attending night school to improve themselves for better positions at work. We all want that extra advantage. We are looking for ways to boost ourselves or get a leg up.

Perhaps this desire, in some respects, is divinely given. I say this based on what Jesus says about the Helper in John 16:7: "But I tell you the truth, it is to your advantage that I go away; for if I do not go away, the Helper will not come to you; but if I go, I will send Him to you." In this verse, Jesus says the Helper is an advantage, or upgrade, to Jesus' physical presence.

For me, this idea has been a conundrum. How can the Helper's presence be an advantage over the physical presence of Jesus? I cannot count the number of times I have wanted a sit-down chat with Jesus in person so He could answer my questions, to say nothing of the times I wanted His physical presence here so He could do some of the same miracles in my life He did in the gospels. You, too, may have wished to live in Israel at the same time Jesus did. Granted, it would mean living without the creature comforts we enjoy today. Nevertheless, getting to walk alongside Jesus, watch Him heal the sick, see Him multiply the bread and fish, listen to His insightful and engaging stories, see Him raise Lazarus from the dead, be in the boat when He calmed the storm or walked on the water—what could compare to that? I would gladly give up my modern comforts to be around Jesus when He walked the earth.

And yet Jesus says it was to our advantage that He went away so the Helper could come to us. How is the absence of Jesus' physical presence an upgrade? How is the arrival of the Helper, who seems more ethereal than tangible, better for us?

Our Companion

Let's consider a few ways the Helper provides an advantage over Jesus' physical presence.

To begin, when Jesus walked on the earth, He was limited to a physical body, just like us. Despite our best efforts, we can only be in one place at a time, and we are confined to the constructs of time. Additionally, we cannot get outside the physical limitations of our bodies, no matter how many cups of coffee or energy drinks we consume. Jesus had these same physical limitations. As you read the gospels, you see there are times He was tired and needed food, rest and sleep.

I would suggest that one of the advantages of having the Helper with us is that the Helper is omnipresent and omnitemporal. He is everywhere at once, and He is outside time. He can be with us no matter where we are or what time of day or night it is.

I find this truth about the Helper comforting in a plethora of situations. When I travel internationally and land in far-distant time zones, for instance, I often wake at crazy hours. I travel in unconventional and sketchy places sometimes, too. It is consoling to know the Helper is with me every step of the journey.

I remember one of my international trips where I began to learn the real value of this upgrade. I was staying with a friend in pretty rustic conditions. We had a limited supply of electricity that was also unreliable, and we had to boil and carry our water.

When I first arrived, I was crazy tired from the long flights and layovers. I was too wiped out to pay much attention to the challenges of our accommodations. But when I found myself wide awake at 1:30 a.m., needing to use the restroom and trying to find my phone in the dark, I recalled what I had been told about the electricity and water. I cannot say I was happy to be in those rustic conditions then!

But here is what I discovered. In those dark hours, I learned to have a candle and matches ready on the table in my room and to keep my Bible and journal nearby. When I woke up in the middle of the night, I would light the candle on my table, open my Bible and snuggle into my bed to share fellowship with the Helper. To this day, I name it as one of the richest spiritual experiences I have ever had. Those early mornings with the Helper were nothing less than divine.

I will also never forget staying at my friend's house in Ethiopia and waking at 3:30 a.m. to discover his wife praying in the living room. She prayed quietly but with an intensity that indicated she was in complete solitude with the Helper in those wee hours of the morning. I thought about asking to join her on one of those mornings, but as I watched her from around the corner, I could see those were sacred and holy moments for her, no matter what time it was.

The reality that the Helper is with us all the time and in every situation, no matter if we are aware of it or not, is truly an upgrade of divine proportions. It makes me astounded and grateful.

Our Confirmer

I would suggest another advantage we experience with the Helper is found in the next part of the passage in John 16. Jesus says:

> "And He, when He comes, will convict the world concerning sin and righteousness and judgment; concerning sin, because they do not believe in Me; and concerning righteousness, because I go to the Father and you no longer see Me; and concerning judgment, because the ruler of this world has been judged."
>
> verses 8–11

If the truth be known, I have been baffled by these verses for years, even to the point of blowing them off because they did not make any sense to me. I recognized the importance of sin, conviction, faith, righteousness and judgment, but I could not see how they fit together. Furthermore, figuring out how the Helper fit into the mix left me perplexed. Now, having taken time to think and pray about these verses, I have a better understanding of how the Helper is meant to be known as an advantage to us through them.

To begin, consider what Jesus says the Helper will do and to whom. He says the Helper will "convict the world." *Convict* here, in the Greek, is *elegcho* and carries the idea of training or teaching someone in a better way. It includes the idea of confronting someone when they are going in a wrong direction so that they change and go the other way. Our English word *convict* has Latin roots that combine the words *with* and *conquer* or *victory*. The idea is that the Helper is an advantage because of His ability to train or teach a better way to live, particularly in relation to sin, righteousness and judgment.

But it is important to consider who Jesus says the Helper will convict. Remember, Jesus says the Helper will convict *the world*. This is significant. It is speaking of the nonfollowers of Jesus.

What does that mean for us, the followers of Jesus, then? Let me suggest that rather than convicting us in these three areas—sin, righteousness and judgment—the Helper confirms and complements us in these three areas. Jesus says in this passage that the conviction of sin has to do with the world not believing in Him. In contrast, we do believe in Jesus, so the Helper confirms that faith, helping us not to live in sin or unbelief.

Furthermore, the Helper confirms us as followers in relation to righteousness. This is a weighty word with heavy religious overtones. Let's take a step back from it for a moment and consider those to whom Jesus was talking when He used the term. Remember that Jesus was talking in John 14–16 to His closest followers, Jewish men who had been with Him from the beginning of His ministry. When those Jewish men heard the word *righteous*, they understood it to mean "doing the works of God." In other words, doing right works.

Let us not forget, given that context, that these men had been with Jesus for almost three years, watching and learning from Him about the works of God through both divine miracles and seemingly mundane compassion. When Jesus talks about the Helper convicting the world of righteousness, then, I would suggest the disciples understood Him to be saying the Helper would confirm, or assist, their efforts to do the works of God.

I find that the Helper absolutely confirms the works of God in my life, both on the level of the compassionate and miraculous. One of the compassionate ways the Helper works through me is through the tremendous honor I have to care for the babies of prostitutes in Cambodia through our night-care program with Saving Moses. A religious person might criticize and judge this kind of compassion, but a righteous person sees those babies as unique gifts from our heavenly Father and possibly the least of the least in our world (see Matthew 25:40). I like how Ronald Reagan is said to have put it: "We can't help everyone, but everyone can help someone."

I also find the Helper confirms the works of God with miracles. I have witnessed countless miracles and events that defy logic and explanation. In the next chapter, we will examine these kinds of experiences more.

Finally, Jesus says the Helper will convict the world in relation to judgment because "the ruler of this world has been judged." For us, as Jesus' followers, the Helper confirms we are victorious and have overcome the evil one because

Jesus lives in us through the power of the Helper (see 1 John 4:4). Because the Helper works in our hearts to help us be followers of Jesus, we line up on the side of victory and overcoming rather than on the side of judgment, failure or being overcome.

When it comes to the confirming work of the Helper in our lives, we can see the Helper is definitely an advantage, or upgrade, to us. He confirms our faith, brings the work of God into our daily living and assures us of Jesus' victory over the world. These are certainly upgrades over the alternative given to those who are not followers of Jesus!

As I finish this section, I have this lingering thought I cannot dismiss. While Jesus talks about the Helper convicting the world, there are also times I know the Helper convicts me, too, about a thought, action, conversation, attitude or decision. Perhaps this means the Helper also works in the hearts of Jesus' followers to remove any residual worldly influences lurking there. Let's consider that the Helper is working to keep us from surrendering to sin, unrighteous actions and the deceptions of Satan, who has been defeated through Jesus' death, resurrection and ascension.

Our Guide

As we read further in the John 16 passage, we learn yet another way the Helper provides us with an upgrade. Jesus says, "But when He, the Spirit of truth, comes, He will guide you into all the truth" (verse 13). This connects to what we learned already in John 14:17, where Jesus calls the Helper the Spirit of truth. But Jesus is adding more into the mix here.

By saying the Helper will guide us into truth, He is telling us the advantage we will have to see beyond the surface.

It reminds me of a gift my dad had in him. He was an amazing man who loved all things historical and artsy. As I grew up, I chummed around with my dad a lot. This means I visited more than my fair share of history and art museums, as well as innumerable art galleries. Because of my dad, I have always been comfortable looking at ancient relics, artifacts and antiques. Indeed, my dad's hobby as I grew up was to restore and refinish antique furniture. He could take a piece of ugly, old furniture, add some elbow grease and tender, loving care, and turn it into a prized possession. He had an uncanny ability to see the elegant potential underneath an ugly surface—kind of like the Helper, who also puts some elbow grease and tender, loving care into us to help us live out the purpose and potential He knows has been divinely integrated into our existence.

Furthermore, consider that Jesus says in this passage that the Helper will be our guide. This term in the Greek carries the idea of leading or guiding a person, similar to the way a tour guide explains to those who are listening what they are looking at.

I learned the importance of listening to such guides when I was a kid and we took a cruise down the Nile River in Egypt. We stopped along the way at various places of interest, and if I wanted to understand what we were stopping to see, I needed to get close to the tour guide and listen.

On one of our stops, I got distracted and neglected to pay attention to the guide. As a result, all I saw was a broken-down ruin with old bundles of stuff stacked up in a corner. When I asked my parents to explain what we were seeing, they were disappointed I had not listened better. Briefly, they explained it was an ancient temple devoted to worshiping crocodiles. The stacked-up bundles were mummified crocodiles.

I was amazed at the idea of mummifying crocodiles. How did they do that, and why? I had heard of mummifying pharaohs and understood why that might be important, but mummifying crocodiles? I would never have considered it. And while my parents could help me understand the broad strokes of it, I missed out on the chance to learn and appreciate the intricacies of that place and its history because I did not pay attention to the guide.

Fortunately, we never have to miss a chance to learn from the Helper, our tour guide in truth, because He stays with us all the time. The Helper enables us to understand what we are looking at, so to speak, in all we are going through, so the various experiences of life do not seem meaningless, empty or wasted. If we do not have the Helper as our tour guide of truth, we will not understand what we are going through and will become the victims of empty pursuits, destructive deceptions and futile frustrations. Without the Helper as our advantage, life becomes meaningless and unhinged.

Our Connector

Finally, the Helper becomes our advantage by connecting us with the Triune God. Consider what Jesus goes on to say:

> "He will not speak on His own initiative, but whatever He hears, He will speak; and He will disclose to you what is to

come. He will glorify Me, for He will take of Mine and will disclose it to you. All things that the Father has are Mine; therefore I said that He takes of Mine and will disclose it to you."

John 16:13–15

In these verses, we learn that the Helper does all kinds of connecting activities:

- Speaking
- Disclosing
- Revealing what is to come
- Giving glory to Jesus
- Giving us what Jesus has

The Helper does all of these things as a means and method of connecting with us. He speaks to us what He hears, takes what belongs to Jesus and discloses it to us and connects all of what and who the Trinity is with us mere mortals.

Let us consider that all of the Helper's connecting work is grounded in nothing less than God's love for us. Paul says in Romans 5:5, "The love of God has been poured out within our hearts through the Holy Spirit who was given to us." The foundational premise for all of the Helper's connecting, guiding and confirming work, then, is God's love poured out in our hearts. In this flawed, broken and dysfunctional world, God's love poured into our hearts through the Helper is a true gift—a divine upgrade.

As we close out this chapter, I will leave you with another poem I wrote in honor of this upgrade and advantage the Helper is to us:

Access

Passwords, decoding and encrypted
Safe but uncertain
Yielding and available
All with eager access

The ultimate yes
Resounding affirmation
We are sometimes scared, excited,
Eager but maybe intimidated

Failures lurking,
Successes smirking
No waiting for access
Always amen

Inspect, Reflect, Apply

1. How could the Helper be an advantage or upgrade to you in your daily living?

2. In what ways might the Helper strengthen your faith, do God's righteous work through you and confirm God's victory in your life?

3. What areas of your life need greater truth, clarification or divine explanation?

4. Think back on your life and look for the places where the Helper was your guide. Did you follow well? What was the outcome?

5. Complete this prayerful exercise related to experiencing God's love. In 1 Corinthians 13:4–7, Paul gives us a rather extensive list of qualities for what love is and what love is not. The New Living Translation of this passage says:

> Love is patient and kind. Love is not jealous or boastful or proud or rude. It does not demand its own way. It is not irritable, and it keeps no record of being wronged. It does not rejoice about injustice but rejoices whenever the truth wins out. Love never gives up, never loses faith, is always hopeful, and endures through every circumstance.

In the columns below, fill in the words from the passage that go in the appropriate column. (I started the first few for you.) Afterward, look at the "Love Is Not" column and think of an opposite word, or antonym, for each entry, and write that opposite word in the "Love Is" column. (In essence, you will be doubling your list under the "Love Is" column.) After putting all of the words in the "Love Is" column, think of the different ways the Helper has expressed those descriptions to you, perhaps even in just the last few days. Look, listen and pay close attention to the ways the Helper reveals Himself to be your advantage.

Love Is:	Love Is Not:
Patient	Jealous
	Boastful

Love Is:	Love Is Not:

My Upgrade

"Do you like upgrades?" Naomi asked.

Of course I like upgrades, I thought. *What kind of a silly question is that?*

We were doing laps in a swimming pool, training for a miniature triathlon, and Naomi asked me this random question as we paused during our interval training. I was having a hard time understanding what she was talking about because I'd just finished three sets of 200-meter freestyle laps in what felt like two minutes, and I was really winded. Furthermore, we only had twenty seconds of rest before the next set of laps. The notion of upgrades wasn't anywhere on my radar at the moment.

Nevertheless, I told her yes, I did like upgrades.

"Well, I'm your upgrade, Ruth," she said. "Ask me what I mean when we're done."

And with that, she took off for her next round of freestyle laps.

"Okeydokey," I mumbled, setting off to follow her.

After our swim training, we changed clothes and joined a spin class to improve our stamina and cardiovascular endurance. It took all my willpower to get through the class, and afterward I collapsed on a bench in the locker room.

"Did you forget about the upgrade comment I made while we were swimming?" Naomi asked.

My brain felt mushy, to say nothing of my legs and lungs, so of course I'd forgotten the upgrade comment—I could barely remember my name!

"I told you that I'm your upgrade, Ruth," Naomi continued.

I looked over at her and saw her eyes gleaming. She was eager to start this conversation, but I was eager to lie down.

"How about if we swing by a park, find some nice, cool grass and take a few minutes to catch our breath?" I suggested. "Then you could talk me through this upgrade topic you seem so excited to talk about. Maybe we could even get some coffee before we go to the park."

"Deal!" Naomi said.

We popped into my favorite coffee shop, grabbed a quick cup and then headed to the park down the road. I found us a spot of clean, cool grass and flopped down. Naomi sat beside me with her coffee and began talking.

"Ruth, we've been friends a few years now," she said, "and we've been through some ups and downs together. Remember when we met in the grocery store, and then how we went bungee jumping? Remember that weird chick who was pretending to be your friend, and then when your mom died? We've been through a lot together the past few years."

As Naomi mentioned each of those experiences, the memories danced through my mind. I recalled how I felt in each one—lots of excitement and fun sometimes, plus struggle, confusion and despair other times.

"These past few years have certainly been full of surprises, that's for sure," I said.

"Before our brussels sprouts chat in the grocery store, were you as adventurous as you are now?" Naomi asked. "Do you think you've changed at all since we've become friends?"

I thought about Naomi's question. Her last word, *friends*, focused my attention. Were we friends? Definitely! We'd been acquaintances while doing our grocery shopping, and then we began sharing more than the occasional hello at the grocery store. Of course, our many zany adventures provided a platform for some really fun experiences. But more than that, Naomi had become important in my life—a close friend and confidant.

Was I as adventurous when I first met Naomi as I am now, and have I changed since I met her? Naomi had this astounding and supernatural ability to bull's-eye questions and depth-charge buried truths.

"Wow," I said. "I'm just starting to get some caffeine flowing into my arteries from our training, and you're asking some deep and thought-provoking questions. I'm keen to answer them because I think they're really important, but I'm needing a few more minutes so I can answer with an honesty and depth equivalent to the questions. Cool?"

"Yep. I didn't think you could answer without some reflection," she said. "Take a few minutes and then let me know your thoughts."

I watched the clouds in the sky and felt the cool grass on my skin, relishing the beautiful sun and the presence of my friend. Slowly, my thoughts began to coalesce.

"You asked me if I was as adventurous when we first met as I am now," I began. "The answer to that question is no. I wasn't. I'm far more adventurous now, particularly due to the confidence of our friendship. When we first met, my idea of an adventure was talking to a stranger in a grocery store. So, yes, I'm lots more adventurous now.

"You also asked if I've changed since we've become friends. With no reservation or hesitation, I would say yes. I've changed a whole bunch, and all for the better."

Naomi's eyes brightened, and she smiled one of the biggest smiles I'd ever seen on her face.

"I'm so happy to hear you say those things, Ruth," she said. "I knew from the minute we talked in the produce aisle that we could have an awesome friendship, and I'm happy you see our friendship in these ways. And now I have another question for you."

I closed my eyelids to conceal the fact that I was rolling my eyes—I knew from experience that these kinds of conversations between friends can get wonky super fast. I was concerned Naomi was going to go rogue on me.

Thankfully, she didn't.

"Ruth, you said our friendship has changed you a whole bunch and all for the better. Can you give me some examples of what you mean by that?"

I took a deep breath and thought about Naomi's question for a few minutes.

"Well, to begin," I said, "I find that I'm more confident about myself—less insecure, scared or withdrawn. Before I met you, I was a fearful and anxious person. I didn't have many friends or acquaintances. I think my insecurity was a people-repellant, like I had this aura of broken, dysfunctional and clingy energy, so people often found excuses to keep their distance.

"Now I'm more confident and anchored. And not only have I developed a deep and trusting friendship with you, but I've also bumped a few people from the acquaintance category into the friend group, all because you've helped boost my confidence and security.

"Also since becoming friends with you, my marriage is a lot more healthy and constructive, and I find being a mom isn't nearly as overwhelming and frightening as it was before we became friends. I'm a better wife and mother now than I was several years ago.

"I'd add that I'm a better employee as well—more balanced and less reactive. I bring out the good qualities in my teammates rather than their shortfalls, foibles and insecurities.

"You've become an absolutely amazing friend and confidant, Naomi, and I can't express how much I appreciate you and all that you mean to me. Thank you, from the bottom of my heart, for being my friend."

Naomi smiled that big smile of hers again. "That's totally cool to me, Ruth," she said. "It's cool because you've let me be myself with you, and by doing this, you've become a better person.

"This whole conversation was why I asked you if you like upgrades. In the pool, I told you I'm your upgrade, and that is totally true. Having me in your life is like the rising tide that brings improvement and upgrades to all of who you are, including your family, relationships, work and personality. I'm a miracle worker in your life in both supernatural and subtle ways.

"But no matter the results you see and feel or don't see or feel, the key thing is that we stay friends. I will forever be an upgrade in your life as long as we remain friends. I just wanted to point out this truth to you when we had a quiet moment for a serious conversation. Thanks for your honesty, for listening and for giving me the freedom to be myself with you, Ruth."

As I drank my coffee with my best friend beside me, having just listened to her deep words of truth and insight, I became so overwhelmed with gratitude that I couldn't find words to express my thoughts or feelings.

I sat up and looked her in the eyes.

"Naomi, I wish I could find words to say what you mean to me and how grateful I am to have you in my life," I said. "Right now, I find myself almost speechless. But know that my heart is brimming over with gratitude for you and our friendship. Please always be yourself with me, and let's be friends forever."

We spent some time after that just reveling in the quiet reality that we are safe friends for each other and that our lives are richer because we are connected. When you're around someone who helps you be your best self, you want to be around them a lot. Naomi helps me to be my best self—she's my upgrade.

9
Gifts and Fruits

When you read the New Testament, you see that the Holy Spirit was supposed to change everything. . . . When Jesus said, "This power would come upon you," it really did come upon them, and they were powerful beings.

FRANCIS CHAN[1]

Now may the God of hope fill you with all joy and peace in believing, so that you will abound in hope by the power of the Holy Spirit.

ROMANS 15:13

Over the course of this book, we have seen many ways the Helper is a divine essential in our daily living, helping us:

- Walk in truth
- Navigate the chaos of everyday life
- Gain immunity against an orphan mindset
- Remember and learn
- Show Jesus to the world
- Upgrade our lives with divine input

These are such practical, helpful ways the Helper works in and through our lives, giving us cause to celebrate at any given moment. But there are other ways the Helper guides and assists us, and some of these ways can be difficult for us to receive and integrate into our daily living.

Have Some Presents

In 1 Corinthians 12:8–10, Paul tells us the Helper offers us many gifts. These include the word of wisdom, the word of knowledge, faith, healing and miracles, to name just a few. Note these are all supernatural activities. But if we are not careful, we can find ourselves dismissing such supernatural activities, putting them in the same category as Hollywood special effects or rejecting them as nonsense or outdated.

As I have already shared with you, there was a season in my life when I did just that. I dismissed the supernatural workings of the Helper as hokey on the premise that they were inexplicable, irrational, unpredictable and uncontrolled. And perhaps that is the real rub for many of us with some of the supernatural stuff—it does not fit neatly into our buttoned-up theologies, mental schematics or dogmatic scaffolding. We think ourselves into intellectual corners, ignoring the possibility that the Creator of the universe can do exciting stuff that leaves us dazzled and dumbfounded.

Step back for a moment and consider the creative diversity of the animal population alone, from hammerhead sharks to sloths, from kangaroos to puffer fish, from giraffes to flamingos. Our Maker created animals that can baffle the imagination. Perhaps, then, it is not such a stretch to believe the Helper can also work supernaturally.

Indeed, the word *supernatural* conveys the idea of something going beyond what is natural or logical. Because the Helper is part of the Triune God, it becomes nothing short of a tragedy when we dismiss the supernatural character and expression of the Helper—whether subtly or overtly— simply because we cannot, in our finite understanding, get our minds wrapped around this infinite Being.

I say all this but also want to acknowledge there is a good chance you have prayed in faith for someone to be healed or for a miraculous intervention of some kind or for supernatural wisdom or discernment in a situation. Maybe your prayer was not answered, or at least not in the way you wanted. When this happens, we can get hurt, angry, bitter or distrustful of God. Sometimes our unbelieving hearts, when it comes to the gifts of the Helper, are grounded in past experience and great disappointment.

We may marvel at the miraculous power demonstrated through Jesus as described in the gospels, but that happened two millennia before we came on the scene. It is wonderful to read about those things—His healing and delivering power. It is awesome to see the way He read people's mail before they even had a chance to speak. We may chuckle when we see how He called the religious leaders of His day on the carpet when they accused Him of being influenced by the devil (see Matthew 12:24–27). We may find ourselves a little curious or twitchy when we read about the outpouring of the Helper on the Day of Pentecost (see Acts 2).

Questions, doubts, skepticism and unbelief often crop up around the idea of the Helper sharing gifts with us today to be integrated into our modern life. And yet I would suggest we desperately need those gifts of the Helper now. They not only improve our lives with a divine upgrade but confirm God is very much alive and active in our world today. I would also venture to say there are people in our lives who need divine healing. I doubt a day goes by when it would not be helpful to have supernatural wisdom, faith, miracles and other gifts of the Holy Spirit given to us to work in and through us.

Just because we do not understand something, that is no reason for us to dismiss it as implausible or impossible. Let's take care to guard against that response.

So, what are the Helper's gifts? Paul writes:

> For to one is given the word of wisdom through the Spirit, and to another the word of knowledge according to the same Spirit; to another faith by the same Spirit, and to another gifts of healing by the one Spirit, and to another the effecting of miracles, and to another prophecy, and to another the distinguishing of spirits, to another various kinds of tongues, and to another the interpretation of tongues. But one and the same Spirit works all these things, distributing to each one individually just as He wills.
>
> 1 Corinthians 12:8–11

With these verses in mind, let me roll out for you a brief description and example of each.

Word of Wisdom

With this gift, the Helper gives us a supernatural ability to know how to use and apply information.

Example: A few years ago, I was in a difficult situation that seemed to be a dead end. The people who were working with me had challenging personalities I was struggling to navigate. On one occasion, I was particularly frustrated because I had no clue how to manage them or what steps to take next. But as we were eating lunch and talking, I had an epiphany. I suddenly knew how to help them work together in a way that aligned their strengths for maximum impact. I also knew what steps we needed to take next. The outcome was beneficial to thousands of children and families for multiple years.

Word of Knowledge

With this gift, the Helper enables us to know things beyond the normal scope of human understanding through supernatural insight and intelligence.

Example: My parents were happily married for several years but wanted to have children. Due to an unfortunate genetic condition, my mom was unable to get pregnant.

They attended a service of a famous evangelist in a different state, and the evangelist called out my mom—whom he had never met, talked with or seen before—and named that she was from Denver, Colorado, and had a medical condition that prevented her from getting pregnant. He then told her to go home and receive her baby. The Helper had given this evangelist a word of knowledge concerning my mom and dad.

Now, both of my parents had tremendous faith in God and thought they would have a baby in at least three years' time. But after ten years, my mom still had not become pregnant. However, my dad never gave up on God's promise, and he never gave up on prayer. And then one day, my mom felt something unusual in her abdomen. After some doctor visits, she learned she was twenty weeks pregnant with me.

Faith

With this gift, the Helper gives us power to believe with supernatural strength and ability.

Example: When I was a young teenager, I had the honor of meeting Joel Osteen's dad, John Osteen, when my mom was ministering at their church for a few days. While we were there, I learned John's wife, Dodie, had been diagnosed with terminal cancer. I will never forget how deeply moved I was in my heart upon learning this awful news. It struck me to the core what an awful diagnosis and hardship this was for the Osteen family.

But I remember even more the faith and confidence Pastor John demonstrated. It was a faith that defied human logic and medical reports. He had the supernatural gift of faith. As I saw him operate in that gift for the few days I was there, a permanent mark was left on my heart that challenged me to grow stronger in my beliefs and weaker in my doubts.

The short version of how the story ends is that Dodie was miraculously healed. To this day, she remains a spunky and perky conduit for God's healing power through her weekly hospital ministries.

Healing

With this gift, the Helper gives us supernatural power for healing.

Example: My daughter, Isabell, fell while playing a basketball game with her middle school team and twisted her ankle to such an extent that she was struggling to walk. My son, David, who is one year younger than Isabell, prayed for her ankle, and she was immediately touched with God's power. The pain left, and she could walk normally and without pain. The gift of healing worked through my son to heal my daughter's ankle.

Miracles

With this gift, the Helper works supernaturally to accomplish through us beyond what is expected or common.

Example: On a missions trip to Romania and Bulgaria in the 1990s, one of our team members, Sheila, had her airplane ticket and passport stolen. Despite multiple and intense efforts, I was not able to get her a replacement passport. I was discouraged. And I was disappointed with God because I had prayed before the trip that no one would lose their airline ticket or passport, and God did not answer my prayer.

Long story short, Sheila had a xerox copy of her passport with her and was able to fly out of Romania, through Germany and back to the United States on her xeroxed passport copy—a miracle gift, to be sure. When I learned of Sheila's miracle return home, I was challenged by God's ability to answer my requests far beyond my expectations.

Prophecy

With this gift, the Helper supernaturally speaks wisdom, comfort, exhortation and edification through us.

Example: My dad loved to flow in the gift of prophecy. He would routinely "bust a rhyme" during a worship service. I am smiling as I write this because he loved to flow with the Holy Spirit in this prophetic rhyme—a gift he asked the Holy Spirit to give him after he heard a couple flow in prophesying rhyme when he was entering the ministry.

My dad's prophecies were firmly anchored in the purpose of providing edification to the hearer, of uplifting them and giving them comfort, as taught in 1 Corinthians 14:3: "But one who prophesies speaks to men for edification and exhortation and consolation."

Distinguishing of Spirits

With this gift, the Helper gives us the supernatural ability to discern the efforts and smoke screens of the devil.

Example: My husband and I were on a ministry trip with my mom in Peru once, and during one of the events at an arena, he was in the audience, praying for people with the rest of our group. Some people brought a lady to him who seemed deranged. People began praying for her and trying to cast out a demon. Reece later told me that as he looked at the "crazy lady," he felt she needed a prayer of peace to replace the seemingly crazy demonic attack. In this situation, he was moving in the gift of the discernment of spirits. He put his hand on her shoulder and prayed quietly, and she immediately settled down. Her sanity was miraculously restored.

Speaking in Tongues

With this gift, the Helper gives us the supernatural ability to speak in a language that is not our own or known by us.

Example: An amazing couple I have known for more than three decades serves on the staff at our church, and together they minister in the gifts of speaking in tongues and the interpretation of tongues. Sometimes in our worship and ministry time, one of them will receive a message in tongues and the other will receive the interpretation of the message. Often, in the flow with these two gifts, the wife will speak in tongues out loud over the congregation. When this happens, we are comfortable to wait for the interpretation of the message that follows.

Interpretation of Tongues

With this gift, the Helper gives us the supernatural ability to interpret or translate the gift of tongues.

Example: Like I described above, the gift of interpreting tongues complements, or completes, the public ministry of the gift of speaking in tongues. When the couple on staff at our church moves in these complementary gifts, the husband is often the one offering the interpretation. The interpreted messages are frequently discerning and encourage and motivate the hearers to follow Jesus with more passion and conviction.

You may notice the common ingredient in all of the gifts described above is the word *supernatural*. This is because the natural environment for the Helper is supernatural to us mere mortals.

I have seen the gifts of the Holy Spirit demonstrated in remarkable ways over the course of many years, in many situations and with many people. In all fairness, I have to say that I have also seen people use manipulation and deception when it comes the gifts, claiming to have supernatural powers, insights and talents when they had none. Despite the existence of charlatans and impostors, let's not throw the baby out with the bathwater.

I almost did just that during the season in my life when I was quite skeptical of anything related to the supernatural expression of the Helper. Thankfully, that changed.

I remember being in northwest China in my early twenties and waking up in the middle of the night with the worst dream I had ever experienced in my life. It was haunting, violent and creepy. Usually, I can shake off a bad dream by going to the bathroom and getting a drink of water, but this dream lingered. I could feel it all around me.

In order not to wake my roommate, I grabbed my Bible and slipped into the hallway, thinking that reading the Psalms would soothe me enough to go back to sleep—but no luck. The dream continued to lurk in my mind, waiting to terrify me in the moments I was still.

I was getting kind of frenzied about what to do when I remembered something a trustworthy friend said to me a few months earlier. I had explained to him I was not interested in anything charismatic, least of all speaking in tongues, because I thought it was all just a hoax—an excuse for flaky people to stay strange and flaky.

He said, "Well, Sarah, when you're in China this summer, you might find an occasion in which speaking in tongues would be helpful."

You see, I had received my prayer language as a little kid. It happened when I woke up from a nap one day. It was not a high-grade emotional experience, with people shaking or spitting on me or trying to make me say things that sounded like gibberish. For me, there was none of that. Rather, it was more like a matter of fact. I told my mom when we were cleaning silverware earlier in the day that I was going to wake up from my nap speaking in tongues. She was polite in her response, but I do not think she believed me—until she came in my room later to wake me up and found me sitting up in my bed, speaking in tongues. As I think about this experience now, it still warms my heart how graciously and uniquely the Helper treats each one of us, giving us what we need when we need it.

In China that night, I sat in the hallway and remembered what my friend had said. I felt alone, afraid, frustrated and at my wits' end. I thought, *What have I got to lose? I wonder if I can still do that tongues thing.* I thought it could not hurt to try, so I prayed and asked the Helper to help me—and I began praying in tongues again, just as I had when I was little.

Speaking in tongues settled my thoughts and my heart, and after a while, I was able to go back to my room, get in bed and go to sleep for a few more hours. From that night on, I have never doubted again the Helper's gift to me with praying in tongues. It is a wonderful comfort, anchor and strength in so many situations.

Over the years, I have seen the gifts of the Holy Spirit manifest in many settings and situations. I have seen people receive supernatural information in situations that were revolutionized because of it. I have seen sick people healed. I have seen miracles happen in families and miracles related to finances and decisions. I have seen people step out in bold, strong faith for stuff that had no other explanation than divine involvement and supernatural results. I have seen these gifts in operation, and rather than being repelled by their supernatural nature, I have become accustomed to it.

Indeed, I would like to see these gifts of the Helper more active and integrated into our daily living because I am firmly convinced our daily lives need more of the Helper. Besides, who are we to tone all of that down in order to blend into a cultural dysfunction that seems normal to us? (More on this subject in the next chapter!)

Fruits but Not Nuts

In addition to the gifts of the Holy Spirit, let's consider that the author Paul also talks about the fruits of the Helper in Galatians 5:22–23. These fruits include love, joy, peace, patience, kindness, goodness, faithfulness, gentleness and self-control.

When I think about these fruits, they sound nice in a general way, and I know I would like to have each of them working in and through my life with greater integration. But what helps me think about these fruits becoming more real in my life is to consider that fruit is a consequence, or expression, of roots. Truly deep roots produce abundant fruit. On the flip side, shallow roots produce limited and even compromised fruit.

Consider that the word *fruit* can also mean "a consequence or result." I would suggest that these consequences Paul mentions—love, joy, peace, patience, kindness, goodness, faithfulness, gentleness and self-control—are the direct outcome of fellowship with the Helper. If you think about it, when you hang around a person a lot, they rub off on you. You begin to speak and behave like them. You even pick up some of their mannerisms. In the same way, the more you hang out with the Helper, the more the Helper rubs off on you, working these fruits, or results, into more and more of your daily living, interactions, values and behaviors.

How amazing our lives could be if we gave the Helper unqualified access to our hearts and thoughts and unqualified access to the community and world in which we live! It gives me such a thrill to dream about what this could be like. And here is the thing. I do not think this reality is reserved only for heaven, for mystics or for hyperspiritual people. I believe the Helper waits for us to walk with Him so these roots, fruits and gifts become normal expressions in our own lives.

Consider that Paul talks in two places—Galatians 5:16 and Galatians 5:25—about walking in the Spirit so that we see the fruits and gifts of the Helper manifest in our 24/7 reality. In both of these verses, Paul uses the term *walk by the Spirit*, but he uses different words in Greek for the word *walk* in the two verses.

In Galatians 5:16, Paul says that if we walk in the Spirit, we will not fulfill or gratify the works of the flesh. The Greek word Paul uses here is *peripateo*, and it means "to walk around or walk beside," with *peri* meaning "around or about" and *pateo* meaning "to walk." This word is used on more than 95 occasions in the New Testament. It conveys the common experience of taking a walk with a friend, walking side by side. I love what this means when applied to my daily living with the Helper. It means the Helper walks with me everywhere I go—when I am collecting my kids from school, going grocery shopping, walking through airports, having difficult conversations and so much more.

Furthermore, when Paul uses *peripateo* in Galatians 5:16, he uses the present tense of the verb, which means that this walking with the Helper is a continuous activity, not something punctuated by events, feelings, people, wealth, poverty, education, ignorance or anything else. We are meant to be continuously walking with the Helper. Paul also applies the command mode to this idea of walking with the Helper here, which means it is more than a suggestion or friendly idea. It carries the expectation that we will comply and obey.

In essence, Paul tells us in this passage that if we continuously walk with the Helper, the works of our flesh, which he outlines in verses 19–21, will not become a reality in our lives. These works of the flesh, he says, include

immorality, impurity, sensuality, idolatry, sorcery, enmities, strife, jealousy, outbursts of anger, disputes, dissensions, factions, envying, drunkenness, carousing, and things like these, of which I forewarn you, just as I have forewarned you, that those who practice such things will not inherit the kingdom of God.

Walking with the Helper gives us strength to withstand these revolting behaviors. I can also attest that when I try to produce the gifts and fruits of the Holy Spirit in my life without focusing on that continuous walk with Him, I become frustrated and instead yield fruits of hostility, impatience, tension and many of these other works of the flesh Paul mentions.

But I also love what Paul says in the other verse where he talks about walking in the Spirit. In Galatians 5:25, he says, "If we live by the Spirit, let us also walk by the Spirit." In this verse, Paul uses a different word for *walk* than he used in verse 16. Here, he uses the Greek word *stoicheo*, which is different from *peripateo*. *Stoicheo* carries a military context and overtones of staying in step, cadence and sync, in the same way a soldier would march in formation with his unit. While I am guessing many of us do not have a military background, we have probably all seen soldiers march in cadence.

Another beautiful picture of this word *stoicheo* is the way I have directed my children in snowstorms. On occasion, we will get a foot or two of snow in Colorado, and when I would go outside with my kids to play in it, I would tell them to walk in my footsteps behind me so they would not sink in the snow or fill their boots with it. Both of these pictures—the military cadence and following footsteps in the snow—help us understand Paul's meaning through his use of the word *stoicheo*.

Furthermore, he uses *stoicheo* in the present tense here also, meaning we are meant to keep in continuous sync and cadence with the Helper rather than taking disjointed, staccato steps that produce stifled fruits and gifts. When we stay in continuous step with the Helper, we live a more fruitful and gift-bearing life.

As we walk with the Helper through life, then, stepping forward one day at a time, let's be mindful of remaining with Him. The more we walk with the Helper, the deeper our roots go and the more His fruits and gifts become realized in our lives. Consider again that deep roots yield abundant fruits and gifts!

Inspect, Reflect, Apply

1. Think about your disposition toward the supernatural. Are you repelled and turned off by it? Attracted to or curious about it? Why or why not?

2. Are you more comfortable emphasizing the gifts of the Holy Spirit or the fruits of the Holy Spirit? In what ways could you become more accustomed to the one that is less attractive to you?

3. Consider your friendships and the people with whom you have spiritual conversations. Would these people be more comfortable discussing the gifts or the fruits? Why or why not?

4. Take time in prayer—not only now, but also with more consistency—to ask for the gifts and fruits of the Helper to be expressed in and through your life with more regularity and freedom.

5. In what ways could you walk with the Helper in greater continuity and cadence?

Gifts and Fruits

Can you come over to help me with this garden project?

When Naomi's text message came through, I knew I would say yes. Truth be known, I'm not a gardening fan, but since Naomi is one of my best friends, I never turn her down—even when it's something that's not in my top faves of things to do.

We set up the time, but when I popped over to her house, I discovered the project was more involved than I'd anticipated.

"Ruth, I know it's early March and it's pretty cold outside," Naomi said, "but it's time to prune my fruit trees, so I need your help. While you prune, I'll collect the branches, and then we can go inside and drink hot cocoa. Sound good?"

My idea of winter sports doesn't include pruning trees in cold weather, but my idea of friendship includes sacrifice, help, sharing and time spent together. For that reason, I said, "Show me the ladder, give me the clipping shears and a few instructions, and I'm ready to go!"

Then I climbed up the ladder for my first attempt at pruning.

Naomi called up to me, "Ruth, when you're pruning, look for branches that are dry, gray or even black. Don't cut the ones that look like they have green on them. And be sure to only trim from the outside of the tree toward the middle, rather than from the inside out."

"All of that makes sense," I said, "but can you help me understand something?"

"Sure. What?"

"Why am I pruning in 34-degree weather when we could wait two weeks and bump up to the more comfortable 40-degree zone?"

"Great question, my friend," she replied. "I took this horticulture class online recently, and they explained the best time to prune trees for optimum fruit production is when they look like they're the most dead. Cutting off the branches and tendrils that are genuinely dead from the winter's cold allows the limbs with life in them to get the full benefit of spring warmth, sunshine and nutrient life coming up from the trunk. I know it seems counterintuitive at first, but trust me—and let's get moving before we get even more cold."

I dove into the pruning fun, fully trusting my friend. She began collecting the dead branches and limbs on the ground, and I scouted what needed to be removed from the trees.

As I clipped, I asked, "Why am I doing the branch clipping and you're doing the branch collecting?"

"That's easy," Naomi said. "You're nimble, and you like to climb and get in the middle of everything. You don't enjoy watching from the sidelines but prefer to be part of the action—whereas I'm not as interested in heights and definitely enjoy keeping my feet on the ground. Oh, and just as an FYI, I have a special treat when we go inside."

"What's the treat?"

"Never mind the treat. Stay focused on those branches and trimming so you don't fall or hurt yourself. I just want to give you something to look forward to when we're done out here."

I thought, *I'm already looking forward to getting warm, and I hope I'm not killing these trees with all of this pruning!*

At that moment, my foot slipped. Although I tried to catch myself, I fell to the ground—but not before slamming my arm against one of the major tree limbs and feeling a snap between my wrist and elbow. When I landed, I tried to bring my arm close to my body, but the shooting pain was debilitating.

Naomi ran over and kneeled down. I could see she was upset to find my arm twisted at an unnatural angle, but she does not get queasy with gross body stuff. I, on the other hand, would probably be puking my guts out, despite having five kids and running the gamut of injuries, cuts and maladies with them.

Naomi bundled me up and helped me inside her cozy home, where I expected her to give me some hot cocoa, call my husband about my arm and offer to drive me to the nearest ER for X-rays.

To my surprise, she didn't do any of that. She helped me sit down on the couch and seated herself next to me. Her next words shocked me.

"Ruth, we have a few more trees to finish pruning, and I need your help," she said. "Do you believe in miracles?"

"Of course," I stammered, not knowing where she was going with her question.

"Then I want to pray for you, and I want you to fully agree with me, asking God to do a miracle and heal your arm that looks to be broken. Would you be interested in doing some believing with me and exploring a healing adventure?"

I hadn't put the words *explore, healing* and *adventure* in the same sentence before, but I had great respect for Naomi's secure faith and confidence in God's supernatural power. Indeed, Naomi wholly believed all things are possible, and I knew in her thinking that a broken arm for God was small potatoes. In my thinking, however, my broken arm didn't feel like small potatoes, so the question of believing rested squarely with me on this one.

I took a few moments to think about her question and then nodded my head in agreement, endeavoring to be more believing than doubting.

I love that Naomi is gentle but confident. I love that she has strong faith but grounded feet. And I know that because of her great love, she has effective faith.

As these thoughts ran through my mind, Naomi gently placed her hand where my arm was most swollen and said, "Jesus, I thank You for forgiving our sins and being our Healer. I come to You with confidence that You hear our prayers and answer our requests. I ask for Your gift of healing to come into Ruth's arm. Repair and restore it back to its normal function. Thank You for Your love and power working now in this arm. In Your name, Amen."

While Naomi prayed, I felt a strange but warm and tingly sensation move from my shoulder, down my arm and past my elbow. It came to rest in the place where the pain was most intense. When Naomi finished the prayer, I kept still with my eyes closed because the warm and tingly feeling seemed to be realigning my bones. It didn't hurt, but I didn't want to open my eyes and ruin anything.

As I kept still, Naomi also remained quiet and still. I think we both knew something holy and supernatural was happening, and neither of us wanted to interrupt the experience.

After what seemed to be a few minutes, I felt the warmth and tingly sensation start to dissipate, and I didn't feel any pain in its place. Indeed, when I opened my eyes to look at my arm, it didn't look mangled or displaced but rather normal and healthy.

I started to move my fingers. To my astonishment, nothing hurt.

Naomi opened her eyes and smiled at me. She had that knowing smile she always gives me when she knows something marvelous and miraculous has just happened. Of course, I was completely speechless. Less than ten minutes earlier, I'd fallen out of the tree and was on the ground with a most definitely broken arm. Now I was sitting on Naomi's couch, whole and well with no broken arm.

"Let's go!" Naomi said. "Daylight's burning, and we've got a few more trees to prune."

I grabbed her arm. "Hold on just a second, please. It seems to me something altogether supernatural just happened, and I need a few minutes to process what you've called our *healing adventure*."

"I know, Ruth, that this arm miracle for you is a supernatural experience," Naomi said, "but I'd like for you to think about something as you're finishing up the pruning job. With God, the roots of the fruits and gifts of the Holy Spirit are infused with divine love and connection. Never think for a moment that the fruits and gifts God has for us can be manipulated, transacted or cajoled with any degree of consistency or effectiveness.

"Genuine love is the root of all of God's gifts and fruits. As we stay connected in deep love and fellowship with God, the fruits and gifts of God flow through us, creating miracles. These are supernatural and tasty fruits, like love, joy, peace and much more. The secret to these fruits and gifts is having deep roots in God."

By this time in our friendship, I knew Naomi would always give me something to think about when we were together. I loved that her words lingered in my thoughts long after we'd been together.

10

Resisting Help

To fall in love with God is the greatest romance;
to seek Him the greatest adventure; to find Him,
the greatest human achievement.

SAINT AUGUSTINE

But they rebelled and grieved His Holy Spirit;
therefore He turned Himself to become their
enemy, He fought against them.

ISAIAH 63:10

"Thanks so much for your encouraging word," I said, my
tone dripping with sarcasm.

I was visiting a church when a stranger approached me
after the Sunday service to give me a prophecy I had no interest in receiving from him. And so with my reply dished

out, I walked away, thinking the guy was a lunatic at best and a creep at worst—someone who searches Google and Facebook so he can pose as a prophet and read people's mail.

I hate to admit the times I have had faithless and arrogant thoughts about people who were no doubt well meaning and sincere who had stopped to give me a "word from God." I have experienced my fair share of genuine impostors, so there is some justification for my cynicism. But I shudder to think how many times I have dismissed—under the guise of discernment but, more honestly, cynicism—something that came directly from the Helper.

I have also rejected the work of the Helper when I have been cranky and impatient. For example, sometimes I am cranky when I return from one of my Saving Moses trips, having seen and experienced firsthand the disturbing and unsettling realities our babies face. A three-year-old daughter selling condoms to her mom's clients every night is one example that comes to mind.

Or I get weary settling conflicts between my kids. Who knew when I had children, I also signed up to be referee, coach and any number of other unexpected vocations? I get cranky, too, when I am skinny on sleep or doing some fasting.

But if someone comes around who is not aware I have just returned from a difficult international trip or have just intervened in the six hundredth fight my kids have instigated in less than ten hours or that I am hungry or sleepy, they may think I am just a cranky person and decide to keep their distance. Because you and I are fully human, this seems like a normal response.

Unfortunately, I think there are other reasons—beyond crankiness, I mean—that we keep our distance from the

Helper. Perhaps we struggle to understand Him. Or maybe we have seen weird stuff from people who are "Hokey Spirit" fanatics. Maybe we know the Helper is altogether "other" and it seems like an insurmountable stretch to connect, so we avoid any clumsy or awkward interactions from the start.

It is my sincere hope this book has helped you cross some bridges in your thinking, and I am praying you are connecting with the Helper more now than you were before this read. But as we near the end of this book, I find it important to address some of the dysfunctional and destructive attitudes we can adopt toward the Helper. I group these into two categories: the unfriendly and the hostile.

Unfriendly Posture

We can carry an unfriendly attitude toward the Helper by resisting, quenching or grieving the Holy Spirit. Let's look at each of these types of unfriendliness.

Resisting

In Acts 7, we learn about a follower of Jesus named Stephen who is persecuted and ultimately stoned for his faith. Over the length of several verses, he challenges the Jewish leaders who are about to kill him. Just before they start their rock-throwing party, Stephen says to them, "You men who are stiff-necked and uncircumcised in heart and ears are always resisting the Holy Spirit; you are doing just as your fathers did" (Acts 7:51).

The part that always catches my breath is where he says they are "always resisting the Holy Spirit." I find this phrase alarming. What would it be like to *always* resist the Holy Spirit?

And these are not just any people he is talking to. Stephen's audience is a collection of high-powered Jewish leaders. He is telling these religious experts that they always resist the Holy Spirit. As a Christian leader, this forces me to stop and consider my actions, emotions and thoughts, evaluating them to see when I might be doing the same.

What does it mean to resist the Holy Spirit, though? In the Greek, this word is *antipipto*. It is a compound word, combining *anti*, meaning "against," and *pipto*, meaning "to fall." It is used only one time in the New Testament, so understanding its usage in a broad context gets a little tricky. Nevertheless, the idea conveyed is an unwillingness to yield. It also carries overtones of hostile opposition. Perhaps it is not so different from the way my kids resist my efforts to coach them at different times. Their resistance expresses itself across a wide spectrum, from gentle complaining to outright defiance, but it is resistance all the same.

What are some ways we might resist the Helper? In my life, I know I have resisted the Helper by ignoring the tender nudges I have felt in my heart to speak with someone about Jesus or to take extra time to help a person. I have also resisted the Helper on those occasions when I have steamrolled a red light in my heart that told me not to do something. (Sometimes I think what we call our conscience is the gentle but steady voice of the Helper in the background, endeavoring to get our attention.) I also know I have resisted the Helper by not helping a homeless person on a street corner who was holding a sign that asked for help. I have dismissed the nudge to help even when my kids have suggested it, justifying my indifference with an excuse.

One of the most consistent ways I resist the Helper, though, is through my independence. In our culture, independence is applauded and celebrated. Consider these words from Brené Brown:

> One of the greatest barriers to connection is the cultural importance we place on "going it alone." Somehow we've come to equate success with not needing anyone. Many of us are willing to extend a helping hand, but we're very reluctant to reach out for help when we need it ourselves. It's as if we've divided the world into "those who offer help" and "those who need help." The truth is that we are both.[1]

Despite the cultural pressure to celebrate it, I know my independence excludes the Holy Spirit. Being independent means adopting an "I can do it myself" attitude. This frequently gets me into messes, much to my chagrin.

Here is another example of resistance from my own life. When I was coming to the conclusion of writing this book, my husband had an opportunity for us to join a ministry cruise to Alaska, where we could connect with various pastors and other ministry leaders. In my thinking, the timing for this cruise was awful, as it coincided with my deadline for finishing this book, so I initially resisted his efforts to get me to go on the cruise.

But he really wanted us to go. So I prayed and was surprised to find a peace in my heart to do it, despite the poor timing and the coordination it required with taking care of our kids.

The unexpected outcome was that being on the cruise afforded me the time and space I needed to focus on the book and finish it—with lots of divine help from the Helper, of course! For several days, we did not have Internet or phone access. There was not much to do but write. Had I stayed home, I have no doubt I would have been distracted and not finished in the same timely way. Once again, I find myself thankful the Helper gives me what I need and not always what I want. Sometimes we find ourselves in situations we do not like and even resist, but they may be just the provisions the Helper intends to use for our growth and even our blessing.

Quenching

A second way we can be unfriendly with the Helper, denying Him access to our lives, is found in 1 Thessalonians 5:19–20, where Paul says, "Do not quench the Spirit; do not despise prophetic utterances." This word *quench* in the Greek, *sbennumi*, is used six times in the New Testament and is connected to the idea of extinguishing a fire. It is an interesting word choice, given what happened to Jesus' followers on the Day of Pentecost: "And there appeared to them tongues as of fire distributing themselves, and they rested on each one of them" (Acts 2:3).

We can quench, or extinguish, the Helper's work in our lives in a number of ways. For example, I quench the Helper working in and through me when an airplane is delayed and I get impatient and rude, justifying my behavior because of the regular inconveniences of life. I quench the fruits of the Holy Spirit by choosing those behaviors. I also quench the

Helper when I downgrade the gifts of the Spirit, attributing them to some other cause. Paul even indicates this in the passage when he says not to despise prophetic utterances and, by association, the other gifts of the Spirit (see 1 Thessalonians 5:20).

I think we are too proficient with quenching the Spirit, particularly when it comes to the gifts of the Spirit. I think we do this for many reasons:

- They make us uncomfortable.
- They feel foreign.
- They seem scary.
- They defy logic.
- We see flaky people use them to manipulate.
- We want to be in control.

But consider what Paul told Timothy, his protégé: "For this reason I remind you to fan into flame the gift of God, which is in you through the laying on of my hands" (2 Timothy 1:6 NIV). Paul encourages the growth of the flame, not the quenching or extinguishing of it.

In my life, there have been several unfortunate occasions when I have quenched the Helper. There were times when I knew the Helper wanted me to give someone a Bible verse for encouragement and I dismissed that prompting. Sometimes it was because I did not want the person to think I was stranger than I already am. I quench the Helper working through me when I get busy and forget to defer to the Helper's leadership. Other times it happens because I get nervous trying to figure out if the prompting is legitimately the Helper stirring my heart. I am being honest with you here in the hope that it will encourage you to be honest with the Helper, too, and so you might quench less and yield more.

By way of contrast, to show you what it is like to surrender to the Holy Spirit's movement instead of quenching it, I recently had the privilege of ministering as a guest on a TV program. Behind the scenes, one of the employees of the television network felt prompted by the Helper to give me a prophetic word. I was happy with the way it all went down because I did not let my first instinct, which was to be skeptical, control my attitude, words or actions. Instead, I locked myself into receiving mode and listened with respect and reverence.

At the end of this sideline ministry time, I thanked the gentleman for his obedience to the Helper and asked him to pray for me to yield to and flow with the Helper even more. He prayed, and I have found myself more open and attentive to the Helper since this man's ministry to me. Not so long ago, I would have dismissed his ministry out of hand. I am happy to be making progress.

Grieving

A third—and maybe the easiest—way we demonstrate unfriendliness to the Helper is by giving Him reason to grieve, as Paul mentions in Ephesians: "Do not grieve the Holy Spirit of God, by whom you were sealed for the day of redemption" (Ephesians 4:30). The word in Greek that Paul uses for *grieve* here is the word *lupeo*, which is used more than 25 times in the New Testament. It carries the idea of causing someone to have pain, sadness, distress or sorrow.

When we look at the context in which Paul places this verse, it is smack-dab in the middle of his directions about how not to interact with each other. Paul tells us to be encouraging and to keep away yucky things, like bitterness, anger, wrath and slander. Paul seems to be telling us that we grieve the Helper when we behave in hurtful and nonconstructive ways, using words that discourage and injure rather than words that strengthen and edify. Let's consider that when we hurt someone, we potentially hurt the Helper at the same time.

When I think about how I interact with people in light of this idea of grieving the Helper, it gives me pause and encourages me to pay better attention to my words and actions so as not to be offensive or hurtful. I have not always approached things this way. In truth, only in the last few years have I been aware of the possibility that the way I interact with and treat people can grieve the Helper. If you are like me, you have people in your life who get under your skin. I find I have to be extra careful with my words around these people because I do not want to grieve the Helper.

On the flip side, I carry a low tolerance for people who talk impulsively, who do not put their words through a mental filter. Just recently, I was noticing a person who shot off her mouth without thinking about what she was saying. I found her words insensitive and hurtful. I think this person grieved the Helper when she did this, and she may be oblivious to this fact. I am taking this lesson to heart as a result of her example.

So, it is not just that we need to be aware of the Helper. We also need to be sensitive to what grieves the Helper. This should be a path of less grieving and more glorifying, to be sure.

Hostile Stance

We have explored several ways we can treat the Helper in an unfriendly way, opposing the Helper's activity in our lives as a result. But there is another negative way we can treat the Helper, and that is by showing outright hostility. When it comes to hostility, there are two ways we live this out.

Insulting

Hebrews 10:29 says:

> How much severer punishment do you think he will deserve who has trampled under foot the Son of God, and has regarded as unclean the blood of the covenant by which he was sanctified, and has insulted the Spirit of grace?

In this verse, the author speaks of insulting the Helper. The word in Greek used here is the word *embrizo*, and it is only used on this one occasion in the New Testament. The idea extended through this word is that of treating another person roughly or with disdain, not in a playful way but rather with hostile intent. In the surrounding context, the author is talking about a person who has been a follower of Jesus who then decides to dismiss the truth he or she once believed. In this context, the implication is that the person insults the Helper by turning his or her back on Jesus. Where there once was tender acceptance of and love for Jesus, now this person willfully rejects Jesus and thereby insults the Helper.

Now, I am sure you have met people, as I have, at various points on the faith journey. For example, during my graduate studies, I took a class about the history of evolution and met lots of people who were professed atheists and agnostics. I was respectful of their intelligence and prayerful about their spiritual life while in class with them. At other times, I have met people who were spiritually curious, and we shared interesting conversations. I have also met zealous followers of Jesus who inspired me to love and follow Jesus with more of my heart and energy.

But the conversations with which I most often struggle are those with people who were once strong believers in Jesus but have since become cold and indifferent to spiritual matters. When I ask about their previous spiritual fervor, they become churlish and even condescending about that season in their life, downgrading their belief in Jesus to an infantile stage on the path to their current illumination. In my heart, I wince and often walk away feeling both hurt and sad. Maybe the Helper feels insulted as well.

Blaspheming

While it is discouraging to talk with people who have rejected Jesus and insulted the Helper, there is yet one more way to oppose the Helper, and it is the most serious and harmful thing we can do. In Luke 12:10, Jesus says, "And everyone who speaks a word against the Son of Man, it will be forgiven him; but he who blasphemes against the Holy Spirit, it will not be forgiven him." According to Jesus' words, an overtly hostile opposition that blasphemes the Helper is a scandalous offense against God that is also unforgivable. It is so important that Jesus also discusses it in Matthew 12:22–32 and Mark 3:28–30.

What does it mean to blaspheme the Helper? The word means "to speak or treat with derision or disdain." It is a more overt form of rejection than insulting is, and it includes a rejection of anything the Helper does, including the Helper's efforts to work salvation into our hearts with convicting power (see John 16:8).

We do not want to slide down the path of opposing the Helper in any of its forms—unfriendly or hostile—because the end of that path is dark, hopeless and painful. Instead, we ought to do as Paul instructed Timothy: fan into flame the hope that is in us, given to us by God.

Inspect, Reflect, Apply

1. What words indicate the opposite of *resist*?

2. What words indicate the opposite of *quench*?

3. What words indicate the opposite of *grieve*?

4. Describe a time you felt the Helper nudging you to do something and you obeyed. What happened? How did you feel?

5. Describe a time you felt the Helper nudging you to do something and you dialed down the volume of the Helper's voice, evading that nudge. What happened? How did you feel?

6. Where have you witnessed hostility to the Holy Spirit, either in yourself or another person? How can you respond to that hostility with prayer?

Change Agent

It had been a couple of weeks since I'd talked with Naomi, and I thought she might be on vacation. But I am also known for getting dates confused. It's easy for me to forget birthday parties my kids want to attend, and I've been known to mix up a lunch appointment from time to time.

All that to say, I don't have a lot of confidence in my ability to keep track of a calendar. But it was strange that Naomi hadn't replied to my recent text messages. Normally, we keep up with each other best that way because we both keep hectic schedules. It's not unusual for us to miss a few days of texting here and there, but we always pick up right where we left off. That is one of the wonderful things about our friendship.

Something felt out of place this time, though, and after several days, I looked at my text message list and realized that although I'd sent several messages to Naomi, she hadn't replied to any of them in over a week. I became even more disconcerted when I noticed I'd overlooked a voicemail Naomi left for me ten days ago.

I quickly listened to her message.

"Ruth," she said, "when you get a moment, would you please give me a call? I need to talk with you about something important, and it would be helpful if we could meet up over a cup of coffee. Thanks, friend. Please let me know when you're available."

My heart sank to my toes when I listened to her voicemail a second time. The second time through, I could hear some pain in her voice.

Even though it was after eleven at night, I rang her number, unsure what I would say if she answered. Thankfully, her voicemail picked up and I left a message.

"Hey, friend," I said, "I'm so sorry I didn't return your call sooner. I just realized I'd forgotten to listen to my voicemail messages for over a week, so I'm calling right now, just after listening to your message. I'm sorry it's really late, but please give me a call or shoot me a text to let me know a few times when you'd be available to catch up over coffee. Again, I'm really sorry I didn't call sooner. It was an honest mistake. Hope you're okay, and I look forward to some coffee with you."

I went to bed with a knot in my stomach. The last person I'd ever want to offend or bruise was my good friend Naomi. By this time, we'd been friends for more than three years, and this was our first sign of major conflict.

In my way of thinking, you get to know a new side of a person if you make it through a conflict with them, so it was important to me to get this situation resolved in a healthy way.

The next morning, I was up early to make my coffee, and while I was waiting for it to brew, I checked my phone. I was pleased to see a text from Naomi.

Hey, Ruth, thanks for your vm, it said. *Let's meet up at our coffee shop. Here are some times I'm avail . . .* , and she listed some days and times.

I cross-checked her availability with my calendar and found an option that would fit our schedules.

Hey, friend! I texted back. *Thanks heaps for your text. I'm eager to catch up. Let's meet at our coffee shop tomorrow at 10:30 a.m. Thanks, and I look forward to our chat.*

Time always seems to go faster when you want it to slow down, but it seems to slow down when you want it to speed up. It seemed like an eternity before 10:30 a.m. the next day rolled around.

I arrived at our coffee shop a few minutes early and ordered Naomi's favorite drink along with my coffee. Then I grabbed a table and waited.

When Naomi arrived, I could tell she was upset. I stood to give her a hug, and she gave me one of those distant shoulder taps. I knew we needed to talk through something that was clearly troubling her.

"Please sit down," I said. "I'm so happy to catch up, and I went ahead and got your favorite drink for you."

"Ruth, you're very thoughtful and generous," Naomi said, her tone formal and cold compared to the warm and engaging Naomi I'd grown to know in recent years.

"I know you've texted me a lot recently," she said, "and I apologize for not responding. But the honest truth is that I've been hurt by you, so it was hard for me reply when it seemed like you were ignoring my voicemail from almost two weeks ago. What happened?"

One of the things that I love about Naomi is that she's not manipulative. She is as sincere as the day is long, so I didn't need to find a cover-up to deflect my shortcoming, nor did I need to hide behind the ubiquitous "I've been really busy" excuse everyone uses to disguise the real reason for a problem.

"Naomi, I totally messed up," I said, "and I don't have any reasons for my oversight. I didn't intentionally ignore your voicemail. I just didn't listen to my voicemails until a few days ago, when I left you the late-night message. I'm really sorry, and I promise that I'll do better in the future. Please forgive me."

"I forgive you, Ruth, but there's a deeper issue going on here than you not responding to my voicemail."

I could feel myself getting armored up, protecting myself based on experiences I'd had in past friendships where conflicts turned sour. At the same time, I reminded myself Naomi was different. It wouldn't be fair to throw her in the same category as some of my previous relationships.

"Here's the deal, Ruth," she said. "I left you the voicemail because I was hurt by something you said. I wanted us to talk about it so it wouldn't turn into something you'd continue doing, oblivious of how much those kinds of words hurt me."

Naomi was on the verge of tears as she talked, and I was stunned not only by her honesty but also by how she could be so transparent and vulnerable without being hostile or aggressive. Her ability to communicate her emotions took me off guard.

I didn't know what to say. I sat there, dumbfounded, and thought over my last conversation with Naomi. We had joked around like we normally do, and I couldn't recall any specific parts of our chat that could have been hurtful. I was trying to process and remember everything, but I was coming up empty.

With a blank look, I finally said, "Okay, Naomi, the last thing in the world that I want to do is hurt you. Over the recent years, you've become my best friend, and I want to learn what I said that was so hurtful to you because I don't want to do that. Please help me."

Because Naomi was so vulnerable with me, I didn't need to be defensive or come up with some lame excuse. I sincerely wanted to know what I'd done wrong so I could apologize and not make the same mistake again.

Naomi folded her hands on the table and said, "Ruth, it really hurt me in our recent conversation when you spoke disrespectfully about your husband. And since I'm being so honest with you, I also have to say that when you say sarcastic and demeaning things about people, it hurts me. Both of these things make me not want to hang out with you as much."

Wow! That wasn't what I was expecting to hear. I thought Naomi would say something about my having been selfish with my time or having been curt and snappy recently. (My sleep routines had gotten messed up, so I had been crankier than usual.)

I had no idea I had hurt Naomi's feelings when I made what I considered to be playful but cheeky comments about a stranger's clothes or the way a person talked or even their intellectual capacity. Furthermore, I was clueless about having been disrespectful to my husband—until Naomi's candid observation. Then it hit me like a ton of bricks, and I began to see from Naomi's perspective how my words and attitudes had been cutting. When I thought I was being playful and cheeky, I was actually degrading and belittling others.

I sat across the table from Naomi, stunned. I felt awful.

"Ruth, I can't participate in our conversations if you continue to make snide quips about the people around you and disrespectful digs about your husband," Naomi continued. "I know it sounds weird, but these kinds of words hurt me deeply, and I find myself wanting to withdraw from our friendship, which I immensely enjoy! So I'm conflicted on the inside: hurt by your comments but loyal to our friendship. I've come to the conclusion that if I'm going to stay as loyal to our friendship as I've been over the recent years, then you need to be aware of this struggle for me and make steady efforts to stop degrading people."

I took a long and thoughtful sip of my coffee and made the internal decision to do better. What Naomi was asking me to do was become nothing less than a better person.

"Naomi, I'm so sorry that I've put you in such a quandary," I said, "and I can see how this has been really difficult for you. I'm extremely sorry, and I promise I will endeavor to change. Please be patient with me and give me some reminders when I mess up. I don't want to hurt you, and I want our friendship to continue to get deeper and grow stronger. You're important to me, and I want to change."

With these words, we hugged each other. Naomi forgave me, and I'm now working to be more complimentary than critical of others. Truly, my friendship with Naomi has helped me be a better me.

11

May I Please Have Some Help?

Helper, please help me to get better at yielding
to You, rather than shielding myself from You.

SARAH BOWLING

He breathed on them and said to them, "Receive
the Holy Spirit."

JOHN 20:22

"We have a twenty-minute wait if you'd like to add your
name to the list," the hostess said.

She knew us well because we would often eat our breakfasts at that restaurant. My dad would put in his standard
order of two eggs over easy, whole-wheat toast, patty sausage,

hash browns and coffee. He was a creature of habit, and once he found something he enjoyed, he would start a new routine. All of which is to say, the hostess knew we would add our name to the wait list.

In the meantime, since I was only seven years old at the time, twenty minutes seemed like an eternity to me. To help pass the time, my mom offered to tell me a Bible story, which was also part of our routine—only she would not tell me the usual stories you hear, like the ones about Noah's Ark or Jesus walking on the water. She would come up with something far less familiar, like the story of Chedorlaomer and Abraham or the one about Naaman being healed of leprosy after dipping in the Jordan River.

While I appreciated my mom's efforts to entertain me, I preferred my dad's Stinky stories way more because of his zany imagination. His Stinky stories were about a talking skunk who would fly with the help of eagles to Disneyland, where he would witness to people about Jesus while enjoying all of the amusement rides. This was way more appealing to my seven-year-old imagination than anything having to do with Naaman or Chedorlaomer.

The truth is, we all like a good story. It is not surprising, then, that Jesus used stories and parables to help us understand many things, including the Helper. Here is the story He tells about the Helper in Luke 11:9–13:

> "So I say to you, ask, and it will be given to you; seek, and you will find; knock, and it will be opened to you. For everyone who asks, receives; and he who seeks, finds; and to him who knocks, it will be opened. Now suppose one of you fathers is asked by his son for a fish; he will not give him a snake

instead of a fish, will he? Or if he is asked for an egg, he will not give him a scorpion, will he? If you then, being evil, know how to give good gifts to your children, how much more will your heavenly Father give the Holy Spirit to those who ask Him?"

I love that Jesus gives us a parable with which to connect to the Holy Spirit. But let us also consider the context of the parable. Looking at the content that precedes this passage, we find out this parable is the culmination of Jesus' answer to His disciples' request for Him to teach them how to pray (see verse 1). Jesus first answers their request by giving them the prayer format commonly known as the Lord's Prayer (see verses 2–4). I appreciate the Lord's Prayer because it provides a starting point for us in the development of our prayer life. It is like a prayer pattern we can pray as we grow and deepen our life of prayer.

After giving them the Lord's Prayer, Jesus continues His teaching on prayer by telling the disciples a parable about a friend who visits his neighbor at midnight to ask for bread to feed an unexpected visitor (see verses 5–8). Through this parable, Jesus is teaching the importance of persistence with our petitions in prayer. In its most simple definition, *prayer* is defined as "making a request or a petition to God," and Jesus' story about the friend who perseveres with his request for bread at midnight is a compelling example of persistence.

In light of all this teaching on prayer, I would propose that what follows in verses 9–13, which includes the mention of the Holy Spirit, further develops Jesus' teaching on prayer. We find that it is a progression—one that moves us toward increasing intimacy and closeness with God.

Let me explain what I mean. Again, the teaching in the larger scope of the passage begins with the Lord's Prayer. This is a form of prayer frequently grounded in religious routine. While I do not think Jesus ever intended the Lord's Prayer to become mechanical for us, it is nonetheless a starting point in His teaching about how to pray. Then, after we move through the Lord's Prayer, Jesus teaches us about being persistent with requests and petitions in our prayer life—also an important ingredient as we learn and grow in prayer. This also moves us into the more personal realm, as petitions are more personal than a prayer pattern. (The man asking his neighbor for bread at midnight was certainly getting personal!)

Then, when we come to verses 9–13, the teaching takes prayer to an even more personal level. Here, we have the story of a son making requests of his father. There is a world of difference between a neighbor who comes to your door at midnight, knocking and asking, "Hey! May I please have some bread?" and a son who comes to his father, saying, "May I please have a fish and an egg, Dad?" I believe this second parable demonstrates the potential we have to share the deepest, most intimate relationship we can imagine with the Holy Spirit.

A Grounded Help

Let's be honest. Sometimes our thinking about the Holy Spirit can tend toward the esoteric. Even the Holy Spirit's name sounds ethereal and kind of vaporous. But let's take a few moments to notice how the Helper participated in Jesus' life in concrete and tangible ways.

First, recall that Mary asked the angel Gabriel how she would become pregnant, since she had never known a man. In reply, Gabriel told her, "The Holy Spirit will come upon you, and the power of the Most High will overshadow you; and for that reason the holy Child shall be called the Son of God" (Luke 1:35). The Helper was the primary catalyst for Jesus' virgin birth. He instigated the chain of events that brought the divine into our natural and concrete world. The Son of God became flesh—incarnate in our world—as a result of the Holy Spirit overshadowing Mary.

Now let's notice another example. When we read through the gospels, we see that Jesus was violently killed and that His death was made extremely public—crucified and hung on a cross between two thieves. We also read in these same gospels that Jesus was raised from the dead and came back to life in His physical body.

But Doubting Thomas struggled to believe the resurrection had happened, saying, "Unless I see in His hands the imprint of the nails, and put my finger into the place of the nails, and put my hand into His side, I will not believe" (John 20:25). He needed physical proof. He needed to see and touch Jesus' physical body again. And so Jesus appeared to Thomas eight days later and said, "Reach here with your finger, and see My hands; and reach here your hand and put it into My side; and do not be unbelieving, but believing" (verse 27).

Obviously, Jesus' resurrection from the dead was a supernatural event. And it concerned His physical body. Let's pay special attention to what Paul says about the Helper's role in this: "But if the Spirit of Him who raised Jesus from the dead dwells in you, He who raised Christ Jesus from the dead will also give life to your mortal bodies through

His Spirit who dwells in you" (Romans 8:11). In this verse, we read that Jesus' physical resurrection from the dead was implemented by the Holy Spirit. The Helper took Jesus' dead body, breathed life into it and brought it back into our living and corporal world.

Based on what we have seen here—that the Helper was intricately involved in Jesus' natural birth and His resurrection from the dead—do not think for one second the Holy Spirit is not engaged in, connected to or participating in our physical lives, too. The Helper is alive and moving in our common days.

I find this to be true in my own life. I have seen the Holy Spirit do amazing miracles, such as healing people and giving direction at strategic junctures in a person's life. One of the times I most enjoy the Helper's presence is when I walk down the road to collect my kids after school. During those walks, the Helper and I share such rich conversation. I have talked through so many situations with the Helper during those walks, receiving direction, wisdom, strength, compassion and discernment as a result.

Those rich and grounded conversations challenge me to accept that the Helper is more involved in our daily living than we often realize. I say this because of personal experience, but I also say it because of the objects Jesus references in His parable about the Helper. He says, "Now suppose one of you fathers is asked by his son for a fish; he will not give him a snake instead of a fish, will he? Or if he is asked for an egg, he will not give him a scorpion, will he?" (Luke 11:11–12).

Consider the items Jesus uses in this parable: fish and eggs. In the version of this parable told in Matthew 7:9–11, Jesus includes a reference to bread. All those items—fish, eggs and bread—at that time in history were common items everyone had in their homes. They lived by bread, eggs and fish every day. Even now, most of us would say we have at least one of those items in our cupboard or refrigerator at all times (if we equate fish, which was their most common form of protein, with something comparable, like meat). And if we do not have those items in our kitchen right now, they are probably on our grocery list for the next time we swing by the store.

Because Jesus uses these everyday household commodities in His story, I would suggest He is teaching us that the Helper is more present in our daily living than we realize. I believe the Helper wants to be a part of our common life, not just part of our religious settings, like church, Bible studies and prayer groups, or for when we feel most spiritual. I am convinced we are meant to say to the Helper on an ongoing basis, *What are You doing in this situation? Teach me to know You. I pray You would open the eyes of my understanding so I recognize how You're moving, see what You're doing, hear Your whispers and notice Your nuances.*

A Sensitive Heart

Sometimes being sensitive to the reality of the Helper means going beyond our comfort level and past experiences. I have already shared with you my charismatic background—that I was born and raised in it—but sometimes those roots made it difficult for me to connect with the Helper, due to some challenging experiences. I also know what it is like to be entrenched in a more conservative or denominational mindset that is hostile to the work and expressions of the Helper. As I shared in earlier chapters, I had the audacity in a certain season of my life to dismiss the gifts of the Holy Spirit as conjured and fictitious, rendering myself hypercritical of the Helper's presence anytime it did not look the way I thought it should.

Since moving beyond that place, I have committed to remaining sensitive to the Helper. Do I get it right all the time? No. One time I bumped into someone at a coffee shop, and I thought it might be a divine connection. As we talked, I learned he was a pastor and that we knew some of the same people. After talking for thirty minutes, discussing our backgrounds and ministry experiences, we thanked each other and then went our respective ways. Did I miss the guiding of the Helper in that moment? Maybe. But I would rather err on the side of trying to follow the Helper's lead rather than being cold, insensitive and dismissive to it.

There are other times such sensitivity has made a great difference. I will never forget the time I first started to travel and teach the Bible and was speaking at a small rural church in the Midwest. After the Sunday service, the pastor's son, a well-intentioned teenage boy, came up to me and said, "Wow—that was the first sermon in two years where I didn't feel God's power!" Being in my midtwenties and insecure, I wanted to slap the kid. Then I felt like I had failed miserably in this small town.

I went back to my hotel that afternoon and pored over a Kathryn Kuhlman biography I had been reading, praying something would rub off. During that time, the Holy Spirit put me through my paces, helping me accept that the Helper is present, no matter what a teenage boy feels or does not feel.

After a few hours of prayer and some wrestling, I felt the Helper encouraging me with words that sounded something like, *Lean into Me and relax. Let Me flow and work through you.*

When I showed up to preach for the evening service, I felt a stronger desire to minister in sync with the Helper during the service, but I also felt less pressure to perform and conjure up something for the sake of emotions or to pacify my insecurity. I kept my sensitivity to the Holy Spirit on "full-alert mode" as I preached, committed to being the Helper's vessel throughout the service.

Needless to say, the service dripped with God's presence. The Holy Spirit gave me amazing words to give specific people in the audience, and I returned to my hotel room freshly baptized in the awareness that the Helper uses individuals, not clones.

Regardless of your spiritual background (or lack thereof), here is my takeaway on this. Let's remain in a state of holy hunger, eager anticipation and passionate pursuit of the Helper, full stop. Let's endeavor to know the Helper in richness and depth—and not just concerning the gifts and fruits. Let's not only know the outward manifestations or fringes of what the Helper does. Let's stay hyper-close to the Helper. I want you to be stirred in your soul with an insatiable appetite to know the Helper better and more fully—not merely through religiosity but through relationship, not merely in the pious but in the personal, not merely through sanctimonious strutting but through snuggly synergy.

A Threefold Way

Let's revisit the Luke 11 passage to learn what an increasingly intimate connection with the Helper looks like. You may recall that before Jesus gives the fish-and-egg metaphor, He gives His disciples three commands: ask, seek and knock.

In the Greek, all of these verbs are given in the imperative, or command, mode, which means Jesus is not offering a mere suggestion or helpful thought. He is giving a direct mandate. We are to ask, seek and knock, period.

Furthermore, Jesus uses the present tense, which means these behaviors are to be continuous. Let me emphasize that again: Our asking, seeking and knocking should happen on an ongoing basis, not in one-off moments or in a situational crisis. We have all tossed up those emergency "Help!" prayers, of course, and while those are not inherently bad, Jesus challenges us here to be more consistent. He is commanding us to stay in the habit of asking, seeking and knocking.

What is the goal of this asking, seeking and knocking? Do we ask, seek and knock for more money, a better job, a beautiful mate or our school loans to be paid off? While those are nice considerations, we must follow Jesus' words all the way through to the end to keep ourselves aligned with His intent. And according to the end of His words here, the goal of our asking, seeking and knocking is to have the Holy Spirit. He closes the passage by saying, "If you then, being evil, know how to give good gifts to your children, how much more will your heavenly Father give the Holy Spirit to those who ask Him?" (verse 13).

As I have thought and prayed about these verses, this command to continually ask, seek and knock for the Holy Spirit has changed the way I pray. It has also fashioned my interactions with the Holy Spirit to be more grounded in my daily living with greater continuity.

When I was much younger, I thought having the Holy Spirit in one's life meant that a person spoke in tongues. But in Jesus' words here, He tells us that having the Holy Spirit leads to a continual integration of the Helper's presence in our lives through these verbs of *ask, seek* and *knock*. This has had a massive impact on my thinking and, consequently, my attitudes and behaviors.

Let's look at what these verbs mean, then, when we use them in our prayer lives.

Ask and Receive

When Jesus says in Luke 11:9, "Ask, and it will be given to you," these words are straightforward. The result of asking is receiving. But let me frame this for you another way: We are responsible for asking *and then staying in a receiving mode*.

It is difficult for some of us to be good receivers. If you are the type of person who struggles when someone pays for your coffee or buys your lunch, you might need to make some adjustments to become a better receiver. Be mindful of the independence trap! With that being said, we are instructed by Jesus to ask and be receptive.

Let me suggest to you the following equation for how we receive help from the Helper:

We **ask** + the Helper **gives** = we **receive**

In this same way of thinking:

We **seek** + the Helper **reveals** = we **find**
We **knock** + the Helper **opens** = we **enter**

In short, we receive help in the middle—always. So in my prayer life, I am learning to be more attentive to the Holy Spirit as the conduit for divine giving, revealing and opening. I am beginning to pray in these terms:

- "Please help me receive well from You, the Giver."
- "Please help me be attentive to—even curious about—the way You reveal things to me throughout this day."
- "Please help me go through the doors of opportunity You open for me today, and help me not beat my head against the doors You've closed."

When I pray about knocking, I am reminded of what Jesus said in Revelation 3:8: "Behold, I have put before you an open door which no one can shut."

Let me give you some more food for thought concerning Jesus' selection of words here. If someone gives you something, what is that something called? It is called a gift. Maybe part of our asking for the Holy Spirit is also tied to receiving the gifts of the Holy Spirit that Paul talks about in 1 Corinthians 12 and that we discussed in chapter 9.

Seek and Find

Additionally, Jesus tells us to seek and we will find. As we think about what it means to seek after the Helper, I am reminded of what Jesus says in the Last Supper discourse:

"But when He, the Spirit of truth, comes, He will guide you into all the truth; for He will not speak on His own initiative, but whatever He hears, He will speak; and He will disclose to you what is to come. He will glorify Me, for He will take of Mine and will disclose it to you. All things that the Father has are Mine; therefore I said that He takes of Mine and will disclose it to you."

John 16:13–15

In these verses, Jesus speaks about the Helper disclosing or revealing to us what He hears and what belongs to Jesus. For me, these words increase in me a desire to listen for, pay attention to and seek out the Helper and what He wants to reveal to me.

When I pray about seeking and finding, I pray for the Helper to make me sensitive to and aware of what He wants to reveal to me. I do not want to be dull, inattentive or distracted from whatever that might be.

I also think there is value in seeking the fruits of the Spirit from the Helper. If you have ever been to a strawberry patch, you know it takes some searching-and-seeking effort to find the delicious and ripe fruit. It seems to me that the more I stay connected to the Helper and seek His fruit, the more those fruits are revealed in my life.

Knock and Open

Finally, Jesus says we must knock and it will be opened to us. Knocking on a person's door has some interesting implications. We all probably know the experience of going door to door for any number of reasons—to sell stuff, to distribute information or fliers, to collect signatures. I do not enjoy going door-to-door and ringing doorbells for any reason at all.

In contrast, however, I get a little buzz of excitement in my heart when I approach a friend's door to knock on it. For one thing, I am hoping they will be home. At the minimum, if they are home, my visit will include a quick hello shared with a friend. It is awesome to connect with a friend face-to-face, even if that visit is brief. Even better are the times when I get to hang out at a friend's house or have them over to my place to chat and connect over coffee or lunch. It is also fun to help a friend with a house project, to meet up to exercise together or to head out for a shopping adventure with them.

Here is an example of knocking and opening from our house. Over the last several years, our family has become accustomed to having company for dinner. We enjoy getting to entertain various guests, some of whom are close friends and family, and others of whom are new acquaintances. My kids often help me get the dinner ready, and everyone in my family appreciates the extra effort we take to make a nice meal for our guests and make them feel welcome and comfortable in our home.

When the doorbell rings, announcing their arrival, I am usually in the kitchen with my apron on, up to my elbows in dinner preparations. My kids will answer the door, welcome our guest inside and lead them into the kitchen, where they get to smell some good cooking hopefully, take off their shoes and make themselves at home. I am not formal or heavy on protocol or etiquette, but I am great at making a person feel welcome and cozy in our house.

The dinner formally starts when our guest rings the doorbell, but I have usually been preparing for their company for at least a few hours ahead of time. I am always eager to have the dinner preparations finished so I can relax and enjoy our company along with the rest of my family.

I think the Helper finds a similar level of joy in the anticipation of that moment when we will knock on the door, requesting a deeper connection and intimacy with Him. Consider that the Helper may have been working all along to draw us closer, inviting us to come in and connect more intimately with Him. Perhaps He has been preparing a nice meal for us to enjoy—a meal that brings more communion, fellowship and integration with Him into our daily living.

Another thing to think about in relation to knocking and entering are Jesus' words in John 3. In this chapter, Jesus is talking with Nicodemus, a Jewish leader, in a private evening conversation. In their discussion, Jesus brings up the idea of entering the Kingdom of God. He says:

> "Truly, truly, I say to you, unless one is born again he cannot see the kingdom of God."
>
> Nicodemus said to Him, "How can a man be born when he is old? He cannot *enter* a second time into his mother's womb and be born, can he?" Jesus answered, "Truly, truly, I say to you, unless one is born of water and the Spirit he cannot *enter* into the kingdom of God. That which is born of the flesh is flesh, and that which is born of the Spirit is spirit. Do not be amazed that I said to you, 'You must be born again.' The wind blows where it wishes and you hear the sound of it, but do not know where it comes from and where it is going; so is everyone who is born of the Spirit."
>
> John 3:3–8, emphasis added

When we read through these verses, please catch that I've italicized where the word *enter* is used. This means, when it comes to the Helper, our knocking will never be a matter of "Ding-dong, nobody's there, might as well go on to the next house." Jesus says the door will be opened—*enter*. It reminds me again of Jesus' words in Revelation 3:8, where He says, "I have put before you an open door which no one can shut."

Maybe the idea of entering the Kingdom of God is connected to Jesus' mandate for us to knock and the door will be opened for us. Perhaps it starts with being born of water and the Spirit.

A Spirit-Born Life

For those of us who want to ask and receive, seek and find, knock and enter, we need to live out of a place of being born of the Holy Spirit rather than born of our flesh. And I believe living out our Spirit birth is cultivated and trained in our prayer times and fellowship with the Helper.

Let's avoid the hazardous thinking that says, *Well, I got Spirit-filled when I received salvation, so I already checked that box.* Another dangerous mindset is thinking, *Well, I speak in tongues, so that's all I need with this Holy Spirit stuff.* Let's allow Jesus' words about continually asking, seeking and knocking to stimulate us to live in passionate pursuit of the Helper. Let's always be asking the Helper, *Where are You? What are You doing in this situation? I'm interested to hear from You. I want to listen and be attentive. Please train me to sense You better. Domesticate me to Your presence.*

We need to be trained in how to connect with the Helper so we can flow and walk together with greater union, communion and demonstration. Rather than trying to fit the Helper into my agenda and ways, when I let the Helper work in me, a vibrant sensitivity grows in my heart from our connection. When I am sensitive to the Helper, then in my heart I am saying, *I'm asking You to teach me who You are, and I'm seeking Your presence. I want to know what's important to You in these situations.*

And the Helper answers. For example, in my marriage, there are times when I have heard the Helper tell me, "No! Don't say that!" When I overrode what I heard in my heart and disobeyed, it did not turn out well, and I needed to repent. But I am learning, and the Helper is training me. I am being domesticated to the Helper's presence and preferences. I pray the same for you.

There is always room in our hearts to grow and nurture the Helper working in us, on us and through us. And at the end of the day, the work that the Helper does in our hearts makes us look more like Christ than we ever did before (see Galatians 4:19). That is the real deal, isn't it?

So let us determine to live in passionate fellowship with the Helper in our daily living. Whether we are running errands, shopping for groceries, studying for a test or working through emails—no matter what we are doing, let's endeavor to stay in continual conversation with the Helper. You can talk with the Helper about anything: car repairs, medical issues, job challenges, marriage struggles, friend issues, traveling mishaps. The list goes on and on. There are no limits to the topic or time.

The main thing is to be sure we are having those honest conversations and connecting in deep, genuine, truthful, heartfelt ways with our Helper. Be passionate for the Helper. Let the Helper move and work in your life. You are wired for this—so let's go!

Inspect, Reflect, Apply

1. What are some of the ways you can move toward a more continual posture of asking, seeking and knocking when it comes to the Helper's place in your life?

2. Do you struggle to receive things? If so, how does this affect your relationship with the Helper?

3. Do you consider yourself to be a curious person—someone who seeks? How does this affect the way you experience the Helper as a revealer in your life?

4. Knocking on a door can be a mixed bag. Think of a time you knocked on someone's door. What happened?

5. Prior to reading this book, how would you have described your relationship with the Helper? How has that changed through the reading of this book?

6. What has been the most important lesson, value, observation or practice you have gained from reading this book?

A Continuous Help

As I considered the closing allegory for this book, I saw two options before me. I knew I could come up with another fun adventure for Ruth and Naomi to share to illustrate the teaching of this last chapter, but I also found myself drawn to invite you to explore your own life's allegory with the Helper—and I ultimately knew this second option was the right choice.

Many of the allegory stories you read in this book originated in my real-life experiences. I dislocated my shoulder once on a ski trip, just like the allegory in chapter 2 describes. As I slid down the mountain on the ski-patrol sled, I tried to nestle into the presence of the Helper in between the sharp and jabbing jolts of every bump we encountered on the way down. I also went on a cruise, as the allegory in chapter 7 describes, and my cruise experience was certainly an adventure with the Helper.

While some of the allegories included in this book are grounded in real experiences from my life, many elements are also fictionalized. However, each one illustrates the daily contexts in which the Helper wants to connect with us.

I invite you to pause right now and remember a few key experiences in your life. Notice how the Helper helped you through those times—or how the Helper may have wanted to help you, if you had been more open to it. Imagine the two of you as characters in your life's story. What is the Helper's personality like? What about yours? How has the Helper guided you, taught you, redirected you, comforted you? What have you learned?

I pray that as you review the different chapters of your life, you find your relationship with the Helper deepening. Some chapters in our lives include fabulous surprises, while others may feel like abysmal failures. I pray that, regardless of the chapter, events, seasons or challenges you have faced, you would come to sense the Helper's continuous presence with you all along. May your life remain synchronized with divine help, now and always.

Epilogue

As we finish up our adventure with the Helper, I would like for you to consider a few final truths. Below, you will find a chart with two columns. The items in the left column describe who the Helper is, based on Jesus' teachings in John 14–16, which has been the primary focus of this book. The right column lists the pitfalls and shortcomings we face when we are living our lives without the Helper—pitfalls the Helper overcomes in us by moving in our lives.

Hopefully, through this book, you have come to see more of the realities of the left column in your life—everything the Helper is continually doing and being for you.

The Helper's Role	Our Pitfalls
Helping	Independence
Guiding into truth	Aimlessness/deception
Abiding	Rejection/absence
Teaching	Ignorance

229

The Helper's Role	Our Pitfalls
Witnessing	Hiding
Convicting/confirming	Indifference/apathy
Taking from/revealing to	Lack

I would encourage you to create an inventory of which pitfalls on the right side are your kryptonite. If you remember the story of Superman, his only weak spot was being around kryptonite—a metal that debilitated him and drained him of his superpowers.

Once we make an honest evaluation of ourselves related to this list of pitfalls, we are empowered to see how the Helper can be a type of Kevlar against our kryptonite. Kevlar is the material soldiers wear to protect them from bullets and deadly attacks. In a similar way, when we "put on" the Helper, it is like we don a Kevlar suit that counters all our weak spots.

As I finish writing this book, I find myself noticing this experience of writing has been an adventure, particularly in relation to writing the allegories. Truth be known, I have never written fiction before (high school assignments do not count!), so writing those pieces felt like a jump into the deep end, and mostly, I had a blast. Linking them to each chapter's theme allowed us to notice the Helper's involvement in our daily living. It is my sincere hope that through the allegories, your awareness of the Helper's presence in your life has grown.

I have also written this book in an assortment of environments. I have written portions in our basement guest bedroom—a space that is spartan, at best. I have written some of it on planes, deflecting with as much grace as I could muster the chatty people trying to show me pictures of their dogs. I have written parts in the mountains, in secluded glory with sunsets that lit the mountains in spectacular, fiery colors. I have written in hotel rooms—too many to recall, but all of them generic. I have written on an Alaskan cruise ship with Convoy of Hope, a humanitarian organization that does awesome relief work around the world. And I have written in my living room, wearing my noise-canceling headphones as my kids and their friends ran around the house in pandemonium.

But this book started when the Helper confronted me about my upbringing and the platform afforded to me through my parents, Wallace and Marilyn Hickey. The Helper worked on me a few years—that is how long it took me to say yes—but with lots of encouragement from friends and work colleagues, I finalized the proposal for this book in Cape Girardeau, Missouri, where I was speaking at a women's tea shortly after an ice storm in February.

While writing this book, I also:

- Dislocated my shoulder on a really stupid snowboarding accident that required surgery and seemingly endless weeks of laborious physical therapy that seemed to move at a snail's pace and continually made me feel I was taking three steps forward, then one step back

- Visited Angola to check on our malnutrition clinics for Saving Moses, which saves babies from dying so they can live out their divine destiny and purpose

- Learned about friendships that provided lessons in pain and pleasure, betrayal and beauty, deception and delight

- Helped my fourteen-year-old daughter recover from an unexpected seizure
- Prayed for my thirteen-year-old son as he took his first solo missions trip
- Visited Cambodia to consolidate the legal requirements for Saving Moses' nightcare work
- Took numerous trips throughout the United States to minister in wonderful churches and diverse situations

Through writing this book, I have learned God loves me more than I knew before. I have learned God is flexible and can speak to me through so many different experiences, including random people and hurtful relationships. I have learned some of what it means to walk in sync with the Helper.

I have also come to accept that I am a writer, full stop. Being a writer can sound romantic and sexy, and there is some truth to those perceptions—heavy emphasis on *some*. But in writing this book, I have prayed I would be nothing more than a pen in God's hand that connects your heart to the Holy Spirit more than you dreamed possible.

Beyond all the things I have done in my life so far, except for getting married and having children, writing this book has been the greatest adventure I have yet experienced. I did it all with the Helper.

Notes

Chapter 5: The Flawless Parent

1. Julie Hwang Duvall, "Being an Orphan," Holt International, March/April 1989, http://www.holtintl.org/duvall.shtml.

2. Catherine Marshall, *The Helper* (Lincoln, Va.: Chosen, 1978), 136.

Chapter 9: Gifts and Fruits

1. Francis Chan, "Francis Chan on the Holy Spirit," Vimeo video, 5:33, from his study *Basic: Holy Spirit*, published by David C. Cook, January 23, 2014, https://vimeo.com/84902250.

Chapter 10: Resisting Help

1. Brené Brown, *The Gifts of Imperfection* (Center City, Minn.: Hazelden, 2010), 20.

As the humanitarian founder of Saving Moses, **Sarah Bowling** endeavors to be a nimble demonstration of God's love in action to the least of these, as Jesus speaks about in Matthew 25:40. Her work with Saving Moses is based on the life of Moses, who at three months of age was almost eaten by crocodiles along the Nile River. Saving Moses works with babies and toddlers around the world where the need is most urgent and the care is least available. To that end, Saving Moses currently works to save malnourished babies in Angola, to administer infant immunizations and birthing care in Afghanistan and to provide nightcare for the babies of prostitutes in Cambodia. Sarah's proceeds for this book will go to the life-saving and love-giving work Saving Moses does every day.

As a Bible teacher, Sarah loves to dig into the original languages of the Bible to inform her studies and bring relevance to her teaching. When teaching the Bible, she desires to bring it alive and to offer engaging and practical help for each person in their daily living.

When she is not enjoying a robust cup of coffee or traveling and teaching, Sarah is busy raising three children with her husband, Reece, who is the pastor of a generational church in Denver, Colorado. Sarah is an active person who enjoys snowboarding, swimming, playing basketball and writing. If you would like to keep up with Sarah's daily blog, visit www.sarahbowling.me.